FROM THE P i T

TO THE PULPiT

JOHN STROUP

This book is dedicated to Dewey Huston,
Jim Corbet, and my mother, Wilma Stroup, who struggled to
raise me as a single mother.

Benjamin Franklin said, "That which resembles most living one's life over again, seems to be to recall all the circumstances of it; and, to render this remembrance more durable, to record them in writing". John Stroup has done just that in this book, *From the Pit to Pulpit*. I first met John six years ago, when he, Mike Aye, and Rick Lechner came into my office to talk about starting a recovery ministry. Little did I know that day what God would do with John Stroup and Freeway Ministries. It has been an absolute blessing to know John and to see what God has done through him. This biography is a gift. It is a gift to all, but it is especially helpful to any person who feels like their past defines them. In John's story, we are reminded that God can take a person who has spent their life involved in drugs, crime, and rebellion; save them by His grace; and make them a trophy of grace!

This book chronicles John's life growing up with his mother and dysfunctional family (to say the least!). It recounts his days as a young man living on the streets, and doing drugs and selling them and shows how he ended up doing time in prison. God found John in prison, saved him, and began to work in his life to prepare him for what He had in mind for John's future. Throughout the book, you will see the hand of God moving in and around John's life to bring him to where he is today.

This book will encourage you, by showing you what God can do with a person who is surrendered to him. John is that type of man, and I pray this book encourages you to be that type of man or woman. This book allows us to look back from where God brought John, to look around at what God is doing in John's life and ministry, and to look forward to what God will do through John and Freeway ministries in the future. I can't wait to see what God has in store for John and his ministry in the future!

Dr. Eddie Bumpers,
Pastor, Crossway Baptist Church
Springfield, MO

INTRODUCTION

Today I sit in an office in the middle of five successful trial attorneys thinking "how did I get here?" I am the first of six paid employees in a successful non-profit ministry. I am co-founder, and executive director of Freeway Ministries. Since the ministry began in 2011 we have started four Discipleship Houses and a discipleship center. There are around three hundred volunteers a month in Southern Missouri alone, and the operating cost for Missouri is close to $400,000 a year. The things that God has done in my *little bit* time in ministry has been like drinking a sip of water out of a fire hydrant. I am now married, directing Freeway Ministries outreaches in the state of Missouri, and overseeing the operations of Freeway Ministries in the states and overseas. We are currently in three states and two countries. Every year we see at least one new Freeway start up. So far there's been seven start up Freeways under my leadership and I've been able to have a part in seeing one launched in Omaha, Nebraska under the leadership of Rick Lechner. I have had the pleasure to travel all over to tell my story, raise up disciples, and preach the Gospel of Jesus Christ. I have a family now and get to watch them grow up in the Lord. How did this happen? I was a junky who knew nothing but crime, and addiction. This book is written to share my journey to where I am today and all the things that God has done in the life of a stubborn knucklehead who wouldn't give up or take no for an answer. There are so many people who God has used to help me get to where I am today!

I cannot begin to even name the names for all the support and blessings that I do not deserve, but let me shout out to *David Van Bebber*, who contributed to the discipleship and reflection questions at the end of each chapter. Also many thanks to *Jan McClellan* for her editing skills and putting up with and correcting my grammar and broken sentences.

This is my journey from the Pit to the Pulpit.

TABLE OF CONTENTS

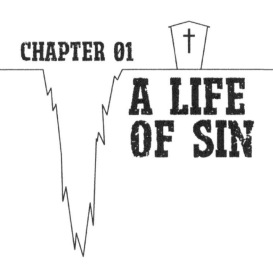

CHAPTER 01
A LIFE OF SIN

Isaiah 5:20 (NIV)
Woe to those who call evil good and good evil,
who put darkness for light and light for darkness,
who put bitter for sweet and sweet for bitter!

1 Timothy 1:15 (NIV)
The saying is trustworthy and deserving of full acceptance, that
Christ Jesus came into the world to save sinners, of whom I am the
foremost.

It's Saturday night. In a few moments I will be stepping out onto a gym floor where I will speak to nearly five hunded people. I will share with these people, as I do every Saturday night, the hope that I found in Jesus Christ. Many of these individuals come from broken homes, lives of addiction, and severe poverty. I say a prayer, grab my Bible, and scan my notes one more time. How did I get here?

As far back as I can remember it was just me and my mother, Wilma Stroup. As a child she was the only person I can remember who loved me. I was born in St. Louis, Missouri. My mother told me that my father died holding me in his arms when I was two. My siblings are much older than I and I don't share the same mother and father with any of my siblings. My mom wasn't even supposed to have me. The doctors tried to talk her into aborting me, but she wouldn't listen. She had tumors in her brain that could not be treated while she was pregnant. She didn't take their advice and for that, I am eternally grateful.

My siblings all grew up very poor and rough in the streets of St. Louis. My brother Gene, who we called "Butch," was accused of killing a man around the time I was three. He ended up being charged with manslaughter. I have been told that Gene acted in self-defense; I really don't know if that is true. I remember picketing the prison in Pacific, Missouri as a little boy holding a sign with my mom and not understanding what we were doing. It's strange that I remember this as vivid as I do today. My brother Carl, who we called "Vincent," was a severe drug addict and alcoholic.

Vincent left one night in a grey t-shirt and came back red, soaked in blood. Vincent was stabbed in a bar fight trying to help my mother while she fought during a bar fight.

Vincent has done time in almost every prison in the state of Missouri. I tell people that I did time in prison as a little boy, just not in a jail cell, but instead in the visiting rooms with my mom. It seemed like one weekend my mother and I would be visiting one brother and the next weekend we would be visiting the other.

My third brother Jimmy was called "Jimbo." I didn't see him much. He overdosed when he was thirty. I have been told that he was smoking crack in south St. Louis with a prostitute and he died from a massive heart attack. The woman he was with robbed him and left him for dead. My sister, Becky, found Jimbo dead in his apartment. He hadn't called her in a while and she began to worry. She was concerned something was wrong, and she was right. Growing up I saw my sisters once or maybe twice a year on holidays when they would travel the long trip to Jefferson City, Missouri to visit or mom and I would travel to visit them.

My mother and I ended up living in Jefferson City after my mom's house, in the boot hill of Missouri, burned to the ground. My mom accused her "crazy" brother of burning our house down while we were gone visiting my brother Butch in prison. My mother was terrified, and as a little boy I remember her telling me that my uncle thought we were sleeping in her bed when he burnt the house down. She always left pillows in the bed to make it look like someone was home. So, we were homeless and starting life over in a city where my mother had no one except a son in a maximum-security prison.

After moving to Jefferson City, I remember my mother working two jobs. She had one job as a waitress and one as a bartender at a biker bar called The Silver Dollar. She had a boyfriend, but she never remarried after the death of my father. My mother was a hustler and she made it work. She loved me and did whatever it took to make sure we had food and a place to live. I love and miss her dearly to this day.

What I am going to say is in no way meant to slander my mother, but it is the truth. We lived a criminal lifestyle as far back as I can remember. I remember being a little boy and watching my mother bag drugs up into balloons and we would take them into the prison to my brothers. Today I think "Man, what if she would have gotten caught?" My mother was a bootlegger as well. She would buy just about anything and flip it for a profit; appliances, cartons of cigarettes, jewelry, food stamps, and anything else she could turn a profit on. We opened a thrift store in Jefferson City called The Treasure House. My mother was a survivor and taught me how to survive as well.

Through my upbringing I was taught that the police were the bad guys and the criminals were the good guys. When I played cops and robbers with the kids in my neighborhood, no one wanted to be the cop. Whenever I watched a television show, I would root for the outlaw. My mother pretty much let me do whatever I wanted to do. I ran with my two nephews David and Keith. We were more like brothers. Being so close in age, we shared a lot of the same history and struggles. We wanted to be gangsters and looked up to the bad guys.

I remember being sexually molested by men and women as a child; I thought it was normal. It poisoned my mind. I became sexually active as a young boy. I am not sure if my mother ever knew what had happened to me or not.

I started using drugs before I could drive a car and was taking trips from Jefferson City to St. Louis to pick up pounds of weed before I was fifteen-years-old. I was labeled with a behavior disorder and it got worse as time went on. I realized that I had a label and ran with it. I was "the bad kid," I could get away with things that most kids could not, and the schools kept passing me on the next grade. I got lots of attention for it. I quit school and began to get farther and farther into the criminal lifestyle.

Within a few years, my mother, a heavy smoker, was diagnosed with lung cancer and was put on oxygen. She received two checks each month. She got one check for disability and one check for social security. My mother got worse and over time she couldn't leave the house. I remember the day my mother and I became crime partners. She called me to the kitchen table with the oxygen hose hanging out of here nose and handed me two envelopes. In one envelope was our outstanding bills and in the other was our monthly income. She looked at me and said, "Son you need to do something with this money."

I would go and buy pounds of weed and she would manage the money. I was in my late teens when all this began and in my early twenties my mother's condition got worse. She made me promise I wouldn't tell anyone how sick she was. She would tell me to lie when people called to check on her. She said, "Tell them I have my days and nights mixed up John. I will never forgive you if you tell them how sick I am." Her eyes were swelling shut from the fluid on her lungs. I would hold a hot rag on her eyes and try to take the swelling down, but I knew she was dying. My sisters would call from out of town. I would lie to them too, until one day I couldn't lie anymore. When they called again I told my sisters how bad she really was, and they came to Jefferson City. When they got there, they saw how bad she was, and they called an ambulance.

When the ambulance came, and they removed her from oxygen, I remember looking at the oxygen machine at the house as the EMT's took her to the hospital. The ball that gauged the amount of oxygen was at the top of the meter. My mother was on her last breath. As my mother was wheeled out the door on the stretcher she had a heart attack. I watched them work on my mother, and everyone in the neighborhood watched as well. As they closed the door to the ambulance to take her away, I ran on foot to the hospital as fast as I could. I don't remember much about the run but fueled by fear and worry I sprinted at a pace I don't believe I've ever since achieved. I almost beat the ambulance to the hospital that day.

My mother had two heart attacks. They had occurred one right after another, and my whole world fell apart. I had no one to turn to and my life became darker than ever. My mother was suffering in the hospital and I couldn't take it. In a short time, her insurance began to run out, and medical staff and social workers were trying to figure out what they were going to do with her. The hospital was going to try and put her in a nursing home, and all I could think about was the last time she was taken off the oxygen hose.

Wilma Stroup, my mother, lay alone many nights while I ran the streets and the bars with women. I couldn't sit in the hospital with her for very long at all before I would take off and leave her, looking for an escape. My sisters would sit with her, but I couldn't. As I type these words in this book, it still breaks my heart and makes me ashamed. Selling and using drugs were more important than loving my dying mother. This was the beginning of my hitting rock bottom. God used this event to start working on my heart even then. I started to self-medicate with things that could not fix me. I became a very dark person that no one wanted to be around. The guilt of leaving my mother while she was so ill, ate me alive.

My mother passed away in 1998, and we buried her next to my father's grave in St. Louis. I remember being so lost and having no answers. I remember the guilt that I had and the hurt in my heart when my best friend, my mother, died. My addiction and criminal behavior went to a whole new level after that. The month my mother died I was arrested twice for driving while intoxicated and I lost my license. I started selling harder drugs, and then I started using harder drugs. I started using massive amounts of cocaine. I lost everything that we had, even my mother's things. I remember selling my mother's bedroom furniture for next to nothing. I lost the storage unit that we had. I gave up everything for drugs. I ended up becoming homeless and I went to only using drugs instead of selling them.

I just didn't care about life anymore. My nephews became very well-known drug dealers and I became a very well-known junky. I ended up robbing most everyone I knew. If I didn't take your money, then I took your drugs or stole your trust. I was alone and, on the streets, doing things that I said I would never do. I found myself risking my life to remain numb inside. I have almost died plenty of times and I should be dead, but by the grace of God, I'm still here.

I have spent numerous times in the county jail, and every time swore I would get out and change; I never did. I did a year twice in the Cole County Jail in Jefferson City, and I read the Bible all the way through. I even called myself a Christian but when I got out, nothing changed about me. I would go right back to that same lifestyle. A year after my mother died my brother Jimmy overdosed in St. Louis. Then my brother along with my two nephews hunted our brother Vincent down over him robbing them. They found him in Madison County, Illinois and beat him in front of the whole neighborhood along with his wife. Somehow a gun was pulled, and my brother Vincent was shot. I was devastated.

I had to choose sides, and I disowned my brother Vincent. In my eyes he broke a loyalty that couldn't be broken. Our family fought together, lived together, bled together, ran together, but we never turned on each other; until this feud happened. My brothers were all dead, in prison, or as good as dead. My nephews, who I loved very much, were also in prison. My mother was dead, and I was homeless.

I ended up in the streets homeless, hopeless, angry, and broke with a serious addiction to anything that would take away my pain. I hated life and didn't want to feel ever again. I did several stints in the county jail for fighting, driving while intoxicated, and not showing up for my court hearings. One day I was riding with a crack dealer and he pulled up by the high school to drop off a package of dope. His girlfriend didn't want him to go into the house to sell his drugs because the woman was a known prostitute. They argued forever over the situation. Finally, I spoke up, and I told him "Give the dope to me, I'll take it in." I delivered the dope. What I didn't know was the house was wired and the police where in the basement of the house watching the footage.

Later, I found out that I had a warrant for selling crack in a school zone. I went on the run for over a year. I was charged and since it was my first felony they gave me probation. I ended up messing up probation and had the police hunt me down. I was held up in a house on the corner of Monroe and Hickory Street in Jefferson City for what seemed like forever but was really four or five hours. I remember the police surrounding the home and clearing out the house. They entered the house and yelled to me through the hallway, "Come out John we know that you are in there!"

I saw the red lights from the scopes piercing through the doorway and I remained crouched on a shoe rack. I was silent and afraid. I was thinking to myself "If they could legally come in and get me how come they don't just come in?" I was accused of shooting up someone's home and that is why they were so afraid to come in and get me. They assumed I was armed. I remember the phone ringing repeatedly and how much I wanted that phone to stop ringing. It was the hostage negotiator trying to reach me. They thought that I had a gun, but I didn't. I thought about charging them and making them shoot me. I thought "Why should I go on living? Everyone I love is dead or in prison, and I am nothing but a worthless drug addict." I eventually surrendered to them and I am so thankful that I did.

Maybe your reading this right now and you feel hopeless. Maybe your loved one is in the same shoes I was in at that time in my life. Can I encourage you that God is faithful? He can save the worst of sinners, and a matter of fact He already has (see 1 Timothy 1:12-17). I will never forget the news team covering the story of my arrest outside that house. All the schools were on lockdown and the whole neighborhood was waiting to see it all go down. I went to jail; and to be honest, it was a huge relief for me. I had no one hunting me down. I couldn't get any drugs and I could finally sleep. I knew that I needed to get away from Jefferson City and I needed some help. I sent a request to speak to my public defender. When I got to see him, and I told him I wanted to plead guilty and to speedup the process. I told him not to try to get me any deals but to ask for the five years that was on my back-up probation. This was even against his judgment, but he did it anyway.

I was sentenced to five years in prison in Fulton, Missouri. I found a Bible and began to read it. This Bible had hand cuffs on it, and the cover said, "Free on the inside!" I wanted to know what Jesus did with bad guys, so I looked for them and what I found was amazing. Have you ever looked through the Bible to see who Jesus uses? Have you ever noticed where God in the flesh went to call those who He handpicked to make a difference in this world?

The Bible became real to me, and I began to explore the Gospel of Jesus Christ. Now remember I read the Bible before in jail, and I even called myself a Christian. It was different this time. I was finally broken, and in the place where God could reach me. In Scripture I found a man that had broken out of custody several times. He could not be tamed, and Jesus went through a storm to get to him. He was not the type of person I thought that God used, but Jesus delivered him. He was an outcast, homeless, and had tattoos in the form of self-inflicted wounds from cutting himself all night with rocks. Jesus turned a homeless man into a traveling evangelist (see Matthew 8:23-34). Did you ever read that part? Have you ever heard a preacher tell you that before? That is the Word of God.

After I read this story this time, I thought to myself "Wow that is in the Bible?" How about the woman at the well who had five adulterous relationships? She was the first missionary (see John 4:1-42). Then I found the Apostle Paul (see Acts 8:1-3 and Acts 9:1-19). Things changed for me as I searched the Bible for bad guys. I found that Jesus used bad guys for His glory. I learned that the men Jesus called were mostly untrained rough guys just like me.

I came under conviction from reading the Word of God. It didn't take long for me to fall to my knees and ask Jesus to be my Lord and Savior. I don't remember my prayer word for word, but I do remember that I swore allegiance to Jesus Christ. I committed to surrender to Him like I did the lifestyle of drugs and crime. I had a simple request for God "Just use me and give me a purpose." I remember saying, "Jesus I have nothing but my life left. Use me like the drugs used me."

I began to spend all my free time learning the Bible. I searched the Scriptures every waking moment that I wasn't eating or exercising. I spent my first six months or so on lock down around twenty two hours a day. My waking time was spent learning from God's Word. I had a supernatural hunger and thirst for the things of God. Nothing could satisfy me but God's Word. I never could read a book before, but I couldn't stop reading this one. The Bible became my life, and I read it like my life depended on it. I began taking notes on borrowed paper and a borrowed pen to write with. I remember the time I spent with the Lord in that Fulton, Missouri prison. It was a special time for me that I will never forget. I hope everyone reading this has an experience like that.

Before Christ...   *With Christ!*

DiSCiPLeSHiP anD ReFLeCTiON

One of the truths found inside God's Word that changed my life is when I found out that there are no good people (Romans 3:10-18). I want you to think about that statement. You might be reading this and thinking "My dad is a pretty good person." Maybe you're thinking of someone in your family that is kind, nice, and has never told a lie. The whole concept of good depends on what standard you are using. See the Bible uses a standard of good that you and I cannot perceive or attain. God's standard of good is perfect. No one you know meets that standard.

When I preach to churches, hold meetings, do assemblies, or share with a small group I share this with them. I will say, "Some of you need to be saved from your goodness. You are too good and need to get lost." They look at me like I am crazy, but the point is made through this Scripture below.

Romans 3:10–12
As it is written: "None is righteous, no, not one; no one understands; no one seeks for God.
All have turned aside; together they have become worthless; no one does good, not even one." (ESV)

Romans 3:23
For all have sinned and fall short of the glory of God, (ESV)

The verses that I have just shared with you should be an eye opener. There is not one person righteous before God on their own goodness. The Bible speaks into that when the Scripture reads "There is none righteous, no not one…" Martyn Lloyd-Jones said these words about those who are too good that they never see themselves in need of a savior, "Forget the drunk, and the drug addict! The worst of all sins is not seeing yourself a sinner in need of a savior!"[1]

Thinking back on my salvation I believe the equality of lostness was a big factor of my coming to Christ. When I found the equality of lostness I got excited. All lost people are lost people; all people are born lost and in need of a savior. All people are born equally lost, but all saved people are equally saved when they repent of their sins and believe in Christ. How cool is that? You may be reading this and be struggling with the depth of your sins and the past that you have.

Jesus came for you friend. Have you ever put Christians in prison? Are you a murder? A prostitute? I have just described people found in the Bible who God used to change the world. Jesus handpicked people like you! You are perfect for Christ to save. Paul wrote to Timothy and he used these words to describe himself "the saying is trustworthy and deserving of full acceptance, that Christ Jesus came into the world to save sinners, of whom I am the foremost" (1 Timothy 1:15, ESV). Paul saw himself as the worst or the foremost, and he declared that Jesus came for people like him. Jesus is on a rescue mission right now. If you have not surrendered to Him, then stop what you are right now and confess your sins and need for a savior. Do what I did when I came out of that bedroom closet with my hands up. Surrender your life to the authority of Jesus Christ and do it right now. He came to save you friend the worst of sinners are worth saving to my Jesus!

Discussion Questions

Use these questions in a small group or discipleship setting. Answer your questions in a notebook following the reading of this chapter.

1. After reading this chapter, how does your past compare to that of the author?

2. In this chapter the author noted not only his past but the past of those around him. How has the influence of those around you impacted the person that you are today?

3. The author noted that he had surrendered all things to Christ just like had walked out of the closet with his hands up. Have you walked out of the closet with your hands up and what does that look like in your life?

4. The author noted his feelings of guilt regarding his past lifestyle. What are feelings of guilt that you have that you need to give to the Lord today?

5. Go back and read Romans 3:10 – 18. After reading these verses do you believe that Christ can save even you and does this give you hope for your future?

References

1. Lloyd-Jones, 2005.

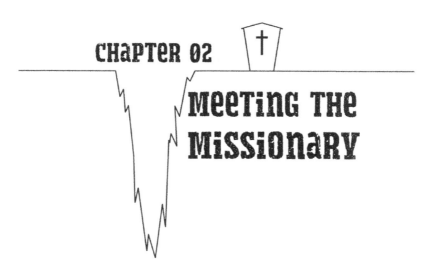

CHAPTER 02

MEETING THE MISSIONARY

1 Timothy 1:15
The saying is trustworthy and deserving of full acceptance, that
Christ Jesus came into the world to save sinners, of whom I am the
foremost. (NIV)

"Like large doors, great life changing events can swing on very
small hinges."- Warren Wiersbe

I was in prison for eighteen months. I had no family to help me, no money, and no home plan. I prayed that God would send me someone to teach me the Bible. God sent me a cell mate named David. I had been going to church in prison for a few months before my previous cellmate was moved, and David moved in. He was a backslidden Christian. David always smoked cigarettes in our cell and I hated that. He and I got on each other's nerves, but we became great friends. He was a wild looking fella who came from the West Coast. He was a heroin addict. Little did I know that David would play a huge part in my life. David had something that I had been praying about for a long time. He had an address to someone on the outside who was a genuine follower of Christ. David gave me the address of a man who would forever be in my sermons and in my heart: Dewey Huston.

A retired missionary, Dewey spent a great deal of time writing prisoners. Dewey had a heart for addicts, prisoners, and the African people. David had met Dewey through a recovery program ran through a church in Springfield, Missouri. I wrote Dewey and to my surprise he wrote me back. I wrote him every week even though I was living on five dollars a month. In prison I could have bought Ramen Noodles or stamps to write Dewey, I chose Dewey. I wanted to make sure I could have a stamp a week to communicate with this missionary. I thought to myself "A missionary, a real-life missionary who knows about God." I had no clue what a missionary was, but it sounded cool. I knew that God called me to something big (Jeremiah 29:11). I felt called and convicted that I was going to be used to reach people most couldn't reach, but I had no clue what was going to happen with my life.

I remember mail call in prison being a very lonely time. I know it sounds strange, but I was in prison with no one to write me, no family, no spouse, no kids, and I would hear "mail call" every day. When mail call comes, people gather around the center of the cell block and the guard calls out names. While people are grabbing all their cards, letters, and postcards with smiles and excitement on their faces, my name wasn't called. This goes on every day in prison, and is a lonely time for many, like it was for me.

Dewey was my letter every week. As I write this I cannot help but cry tears of joy, and sadness remembering that feeling of loneliness. I want to encourage the retired person who feels like their ministry is over to think on the impact you can have for the kingdom by simply writing a few sentences to a convict without someone on the outside who cares. You can be used still, friends, if you allow Him to use you.

God used those letters and that man of God to rescue me from loneliness. God used Dewey to make me see that God had people who loved me in this world. I read those letters and I shared them with everyone in the cellblock that would read them. The letters were very personal and full of Bible studies. Today, ten years later, as a pastor in ministry, I write prisoners on a weekly basis. I will never forget those letters Dewey wrote me. Out of all the men and women God has used to impact my life, Dewey Huston stands at the top of them all, and much of that has to do with the time he took to write me back.

I read about great missionaries of old like David Livingstone, and I am reminded of Dewey. David

Livingstone died beside his cot, kneeling in prayer and though his body was shipped back home from Africa, the natives cut out his heart and buried it there on the mission field of Africa before sending it back for burial.[2] The people of Africa knew that even though he was from England his heart was on the mission field of Africa.[3] Like Livingstone, Dewey Huston was one of a kind. He was misunderstood, and many thought he was wasting his time, but they were all wrong.

Dewey had never had a drop of drugs or alcohol, but his heart was buried with this people group. Dewey and I developed a great relationship through the mail. I felt like I knew him though we had yet to meet in person. I made a commitment to the Lord that I would not go back to where I was from. And little did I know Dewey would be a vessel used by God to help me find my way to Springfield, Missouri.

I ended up getting released from prison in 2009. Dewey wrote me a reference letter to help me get into a men's transitional housing in the middle of nowhere. I tried to find a job but there was no work anywhere to be found. I remember walking the hills and the fog being so thick that I thought I would get hit by a car looking for work. The driveway of the men's housing ended at a T in the highway. Regardless of if I turned left or right it was three miles plus to civilization; Steelville, Missouri on the right and Cuba, Missouri on the left. I begged for work, and I would walk every day praying that I would not get run over and that God would help me find a job. The organization that was housing me took us over an hour away down the highway to Rolla, Missouri. They would drop us off and leave us to look for work. I was broke, hungry, and discouraged about work. Little did I know that God was protecting me and keeping me from a job that would hinder me from coming to Springfield, Missouri. Today I thank God I didn't have a job, because that may have very likely kept me from coming to where I am today.

I never called Dewey from prison nor did I ask him for any money. I was so thankful for him writing me and being a part of my life. I will never forget what Dewey told me after I called him to say thanks. Dewey said "John, I have written prisoners for 13 years and you are the first person to find me and say thank you." Talk about commitment. Can you believe that? I cannot believe he continued that long with no one to thank him. Not one person. Seriously? That is the type of person Dewey Huston was.

I have an understanding now of his level of commitment, but it is still hard to swallow. Dewey came to Cuba, Missouri and took me to Springfield in September 2009 to try and find another place to start my life over. I was accepted into the Salvation Army. There was one issue though, my Parole Officer only gave me permission to travel to Springfield, Missouri to see if I could find a place of residence, but he never gave me permission to move there. Dewey had no clue about the seriousness of changing residency while on parole without permission.

I remember it was later in the afternoon when Dewey said "John, I cannot come back again and pick you up tomorrow. You are going to have to pack up today or stay at the program you are in." I kept calling and calling the Parole Office asking to speak to my officer. My Parole Officer was out of the office and in court. It was getting later and later in the day. I knew that soon enough it would be too late to reach him in his office. I remember thinking "I just got out of prison and I cannot get a violation on my probation."

As we got closer to the half-way house I was staying in, I remember thinking "What am I going to do?" I knew that this was a one-shot deal with Dewey, and if he left me, I had no ride back to Springfield. I had been accepted into the Salvation Army, but I couldn't check in until the next day. It was past 5:00 p.m. and I knew there was no way that the Parole Officer was going to be at his office that late in the day. Then Dewey's phone rang. Dewey answered the phone and said, "Hold on just a second" and he handed me the phone. It was my Parole Officer and he was calling me from his home phone to give me permission to move. Can you believe that? I couldn't believe it! I was shouting out loud and crying at the same time. I remember being thirty minutes away from the house I was living in when that phone call came in. Parole Officers don't normally do stuff like that with clients fresh out of prison, but He did it that day friends.

Since I couldn't go to the Salvation Army that night Dewey took me home to his house. I spent my first night in Springfield on the living room floor of Dewey and Connie

Huston's house. Consider this: What are the odds? I was placed with my old cell mate David. He had the name of a person who was faithful to write to me every week and answer my questions. I never planned on moving to Springfield and I never planned to meet Dewey in person. God had another plan. There I was walking into the home of the missionary that wrote me those letters. There I was walking into the God ordained plan for my life.

You should have seen the look on Connie Huston's face when she saw Dewey bring me home that night. He had been gone all day and then he brings me in and says "Connie, this is John Stroup and he is staying the night with us." She was so shocked and the shock was evident on her face. She looked at me like "He is going to kill both of us in our sleep." She made me dinner and then made me a pallet on the floor like a grandmother would her grandson. I remember watching the ceiling fan spin in the middle of the night thinking "God put me here, and I wonder what He is going to do with me?"

I was probably more afraid than Ms. Connie. My fear was that I would fail. I was overwhelmed, insecure, out of place, but prayed for God to give me peace. I sought God through the fear and insecurities. He is so faithful. I had no idea what was next -- but as my friend Rick Lechner says, I was ready to do "the next right thing." God was about to take me on a journey of trials, tribulations, amazements, adventures, and show me just how much He can do through the foolish things of this world (1 Corinthians 1:18).

DiSCiPLeSHiP anD ReFLeCTiOn

The Bible speaks of God using the foolish things of this world. Do you really believe that? Read 1 Corinthians 1:18-31. Now spend some time reflecting on that Scripture. I believe as I write this that God is waiting for someone to respond in faith to His promises. Honestly, I was just too stubborn to *not* believe the truth about what God's Word says about me.

What plans have you made that God interrupted? Think about all the times that you thought you knew what God wanted you to do. God's declares His ways are not our ways, and our plans are not always what we think they are (Isaiah 55:8). Read these verses and think about your relationship with the Lord.

Isaiah 55:8
Proverbs 19:1
Proverbs 16:9

DISCUSSION QUESTIONS

Use these questions in a small group or discipleship setting. Answer your questions in a notebook following the reading of this chapter.

1. How has God's ways not lined up with your ways?

2. How has God exchanged your plans for His? I don't know about you, but I am thankful for God's sovereignty today.

3. If you could have written out where you would be last year, do you think today the events in the twelve months would match your plans?

4. Dewey and Connie took a risk for the good of the kingdom; it displayed their love for the Lord in an amazing way. Can you identify those who have taken a risk for you and what have been the impacts of those actions on you?

5. I feared what the future had in store for me but at the same time I trusted the Lord to direct my path. What fears do you have about the future? How are you going to face those fears?

References

1. Wiersbe, Warren W., The Wiersbe Bible Commentary: the Complete Old Testament in One Volume. David C. Cook, 2007.

2. Galli, M., & Olsen, T. (2000). Introduction. In 131 Christians everyone should know (p. 247). Nashville, TN: Broadman & Holman Publishers.

3. Ibid.

CHAPTER 03

HOME IS WHEREVER YOU LAY YOUR HEAD

Proverbs 3:5–6
Trust in the Lord with all your heart,
and do not lean on your own understanding.
In all your ways acknowledge Him,
and He will make straight your paths. (ESV)

Matthew 6:33
But seek first the kingdom of God and His righteousness,
and all these things will be added to you. (ESV)

The next day I woke up on the floor of Dewey Huston's home. I remember being the first person awake and praying to God for strength. Dewey dropped me off and gave me ten dollars. I will never forget him handing me that money and saying, "Here is some money, you might need it." Above the door of the shelter were the words "Where Jesus is the way of life . . ." I felt like I was in a different country. I didn't know the language, the landscape, or the people. I was starting my whole life over, at the age of thirty three, in a place I had never been. I had no family that I was close to in the free world, but I had my faith in Christ. I was dressed in some hand me downs but I had joy knowing that God had done so much for me. I remember being very out of place in the Salvation Army. I lived in a huge open bay with 25 street people and had no clue about Springfield. The building was huge with a chapel inside and had a Pentecostal preacher, Rev. Jim Snell, who was always fired up and ready to preach the Gospel.

I remember my first day job hunting and many of the others inside the shelter being lazy and sitting back watching me getting ready to hit the streets and look for work. "There are no jobs out there we have looked everywhere" they would say. I thought to myself "God will open doors no one can open and close doors no one can shut." I was on a mission and believed that God was going to make a way. I had no clue where to look for work, but I found out where the bus station was and hit the streets with hope. I had a chore to do every day and I made sure I got it done. After finishing up I was on the bus looking for work. I was a door knocker, friends. I asked the bus driver "What areas are there restaurants and businesses?" Then I had them drop me off at those places. I could not use a computer, so I had to get my applications in person. I remember being cold, tired, hungry, thirsty, and dealing with it; I refused to quit.

My favorite spiel to an employer was "Give me a job that no one wants, and I will do that better than anyone has ever done it." I didn't give into the doubt and negativity because I knew that God blesses obedience. In the past I had done some restaurant work and I loved to cook. Being raised by a single mom I was in the kitchen with her a lot helping her cook. Cooking is what I hoped to do but I didn't start out cooking because God had another plan. I got a job and was the happiest bell ringer in Springfield. Do you know what a bell ringer is? They stand out in front of businesses with a kettle and ring a bell asking for donations. That was my first job as a free man and even in the freezing cold I had joy.

I remember standing outside of different businesses and having so much hope for the future. Looking back now I know that it was the Lord encouraging me through it all. One day I was standing outside of the Battlefield Mall in Springfield ringing a bell for the Salvation Army when I noticed that there was some construction going on inside the mall. I had heard a guy say it was going to be a restaurant. I remember construction workers going in and out of the building. The windows were boarded up and you could hear them working from the corner of the mall where I stood at my kettle.

Living at the Salvation Army, I had a locker assigned to me but couldn't keep food. With no money, I was dependent on the food the shelter provided. I had a baloney sandwich, an apple, and a thirty-minute break. I could eat my sandwich or investigate that boarded up building. I just knew that I should try and get a job there. As I walked through the door, there were people working all over the place. Honestly, you wouldn't know it was going to be a restaurant by the looks of the construction. When I walked into the building I asked one of the construction workers "Where is the owner of the restaurant?" "In the back," was his reply. I walked into the back through the doors and down a hallway and ran right into Mona Wagner. Here I was, a homeless man dressed in hand me downs standing face-to-face with an executive business owner from Montana.

I told Mona "I know that I look like I need to be on a most wanted poster somewhere, but I am a born-again believer in Jesus Christ. I just need a chance. Give me a job no one wants, and I will do it better than anyone has ever done it." She gave me an application. I came back a week later and got the job. That began my relationship with Mona and Leron Wagner. I know it doesn't make sense to get an application when you have snot frozen to your face and you look halfway homeless. God isn't into what make sense to people and my life is evidence of that. I am telling you when God leads you to do something, you do it regardless of what may or may not make sense.

Mona and Leron became like a mother and father to me. What I found out later blew me away. The general manager of that restaurant told Mona he would not hire me and that she was making a mistake. Mona told him he didn't have a choice and he better hire me or else. She fought for me and months later that manager was fired. By this time, I was a few months into the job, and my relationship with Mona and Leron developed into something very special. I shared my testimony with them. For some reason sharing my testimony and living in a shelter wasn't as embarrassing as it may seem to most. I developed a strong bond with them because God was working out a bigger picture than I could have ever imagined.

I remember watching others at that restaurant pass me up when I was working harder than them. I knew that I was working harder than them, and I should have, in my opinion, been promoted before they were. I began to look for another job on my free time. I hit the city bus again and I found a position at another restaurant. So, I applied at another restaurant and had a job offer. I gave my notice and they countered with a salaried position as the kitchen manager. I was so amazed but also knew I had to pray about what to do. According to the shelter rules, I couldn't work nights. I talked with the Pastor of the shelter and told him I would have to find another place to live due to the position requiring me to work nights. The Pastor changed the rules for me so that I would not leave the program. Can you believe that? He made an exception for me to keep me there. Please listen to me, especially if you are reading this and settling for less than what you should get. The best time to find a job is when you have one. Do not settle for less or be satisfied with a job when

you know you can do better. I tell that to our disciples at
Freeway Ministries all the time.

I was a homeless man,
living in a shelter, five months
out of prison and I was riding
that same old city bus. I was
also running a kitchen and I
didn't even know how to turn
the computer on to do the food
orders. I was saving all my

money and I was wondering what God's plan was for my life.
Have you ever been there? I remember having time to think
at the bus stop every morning and evening as I waited on my
bus to come. I had an MP3 player full of worship music that
one of my buddies at the shelter gave me, and I would turn it
up and weep thinking of God's perfect plan for me.

My mind was full of what was to come. I remember it
being cold and leaving that restaurant late at night walking to
the city bus. All the other employees were driving their cars
home, and I was waiting at the bus stop for my bus
wondering what was going to happen to my life. The special
bonds I made with people at that restaurant were nothing
short of a miracle.

Mona and Leron came to Springfield, when their son
came here for college. They had no family in Springfield. They
were at a church service when the Lord burdened them to
stay in the city. Leron says that it was overwhelming. He said
he was weeping in that service and the next thing you know

they found out that there was building for lease perfect for a restaurant. They owned a franchised restaurant already in Montana and decided to investigate opening one in Springfield. The next thing you know they were leasing this huge space at the mall in Springfield, Missouri. Their son moved back to Montana and they stayed in Springfield.

Who could have planned that the owners of this restaurant were far away from any of their family as well? It was a perfect fit. If that wasn't enough, they were also Christians. We would pray together, shared the Gospel with each other, and had great fellowship. As time goes on, I would see how God used this relationship, and others in detailed ways for His kingdom. He was right there in the middle of all of it. As I look back I see clearly it now.

I cannot help but think "What would have happened if I didn't go in that restaurant?" "What would have happened if David didn't come into that old dirty prison cell that day?" Think about that for a minute. God placed me at that Salvation Army kettle on that cold day outside of that restaurant. It was all done by His sovereign plan. God used those moments all as part of His plan, and I don't have to understand it. All a person needs to do is be obedient as the Lord leads, and trust Him.

DISCIPLESHIP AND REFLECTIONS

Earlier on in this chapter you read about those who were lazy and trying to discourage me from looking for work. Even though it was 2009 and there was a serious lack of work and our economy was not doing well, but God had a job for me. I want you to think about the sin of being lazy and think about the harm it causes people. Has God ever used a lazy person to do anything? Reading my Bible daily since I have been saved I have yet to see anywhere that God calls a lazy person for His work. Read these verses in Proverbs 10:4; 12:11, 24; 13:4 and see what God says about being lazy. This pertains, in my opinion, to the study of God's Word as well as working. God calls us to be diligent in all things.

DISCUSSION QUESTIONS

Use these questions in a small group or discipleship setting. Answer your questions in a notebook following the reading of this chapter.

1. In what ways has God blessed you when you became diligent? How can you relate to people who tried to discourage you from being diligent due to their laziness?

2. Throughout this book you will see the handy work of the Lord through His sovereignty. One of the chief attributes that makes God holy is His sovereignty in everything. In what ways do you see faith in the sovereignty of God as a benefit to the follower of Christ?

3. John Wesley said, "Show me a worm that can understand a man, and I will show you a man who can understand God."[1] Trusting in God's plan for your life will help you focus on being faithful in the *right now* instead of being distracted by the *tomorrow*. Read Matthew 6:25-34, Proverbs 3:5-6 and meditate on those Scriptures for a moment. Notice what Jesus promised if we would seek God's kingdom first, then

all these other things would be added and provided just like God provides for everything else.

4. I took some risk that ended up being part of God's plan for my life. What are some risks that you will have to take as part of God's plan for you?

5. Often when I stood at the bus stop watching others drive away from work in their cars I faced comparing myself to others. I battled this with reflecting on God's plan for me and filling my head with worship music. How are you going to prepare yourself when the temptation of comparing yourself to others comes?

REFERENCES

1. "Christian Quotes." Christianity Christian Quotes, christian-quotes.christian.com/.

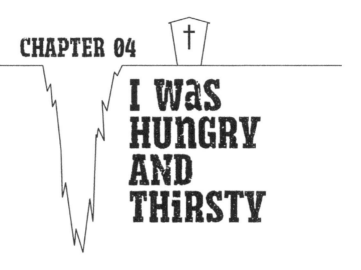

CHAPTER 04

I WAS HUNGRY AND THIRSTY

Matthew 5:6
"Blessed are those who hunger and
thirst for righteousness, for they shall be satisfied." (ESV)

Luke 9:62
Jesus said to him, "No one who puts his hand to the plow
and looks back is fit for the kingdom of God." (ESV)

Growing up, I was known as Big John. My mom called me the human garbage disposal. I would eat anything, and everything placed in front of me. One thing I cannot eat is hominy. I found that out in prison. I remember being so hungry and seeing food on people's plates that they didn't eat, and I would say "Don't throw that away! I will eat it!" unless it was hominy.

I tried everything to make it edible. I mixed it with gravy, mashed potatoes, meat, and everything else on my prison tray. Nothing I did could make me like hominy. I wasn't hungry enough to eat hominy. But there is a different kind of hunger, one that comes from God. A hunger for righteousness that will drive a person to learn and grow in the Lord. I hope it helps you understand the new nature a person obtains when they become a Christian.

Warren Wiersbe describes the new nature developing in a new Christian in three very important characteristics. The new nature depicts appetite, environment, and association. I know of no better way to describe it than that. I became hungry for things that this world *couldn't* offer.

This hunger began under the leadership of an old Pentecostal preacher who served as a Chaplain in the Missouri Department of Corrections for 12 years. His name was Jim Snell, and he was a short, fiery fella who wasn't afraid of anyone. Jim

John and Jim Snell

Snell was an ex-drunk who had been abusive to his wife for years before coming to the Lord. Jim was a pistol and had a reputation for being tough, rough, and strait forward. There have been lots of people who complained about Pastor Jim, but I loved Jim and he had a big part to do with teaching me how to be a leader.

Pastor Jim ran the Salvation Army men's program for over eleven years with a dynamic structure. We would have study time in the mornings with our Bibles when we weren't working. I remember brother Jim would be sitting in front of the men at a table and he would be studying his Bible. Then we would have a lesson. He was the first person to see me as a preacher and gave me some opportunities to share at the shelter. I remember seeking out any and everything that I could be a part of to improve who I was. I would sign up for any class, meeting, event, or program that would help me better myself. I probably drove Brother Snell crazy knocking on his office door during the day as I studied my Bible.

I began to preach the Gospel anywhere I could. I knew that God called me to be a preacher before I had a clue how to prepare a sermon, or what it really meant to handle God's Word. I started at the church that Dewy belonged to. He was the missionary that wrote me while I was in prison. He had a little book store inside the foyer of the church he was part of. Dewey was very active in the ministries there at the church. I went every chance I could without making any excuses on why I could not attend. There is nothing in the world that would keep me from attending classes, Bible studies, men's breakfast, or whatever I could be a part of. I was hungry for more, and I wanted to grow in the Lord more than anything. I know now that this was a supernatural work of the Lord inside of me (Romans 8:8).

This part of my life I always share with those who live in the Freeway Ministries Discipleship Houses. I explain to them "What could have stopped you from getting high or drunk when you were in addiction? Nothing! Then place that same effort into pursuing the Lord and learning to follow Christ, and you will be successful." I was not going to miss church for anything. I wouldn't let anything keep me from getting high, so why would I let anything keep me from pursuing the Lord? So what if I had to walk ten miles? That is what I would have to do to get it done. Honestly, I never had to walk ten miles to get to church, but I would have.

I do not promote a sinful lifestyle in anyway, but the drive I had to live that lifestyle was unstoppable. The same motivation to the lifestyle of addiction and crime was now transformed into the motivation to live for Christ. I knew that the same type of drive was needed to do what needed to be done in my life. I learned the rules of the program I was living in and made sure I followed them thoroughly. Constantly, I was on the hunt to learn and better myself. I wanted to be different, I needed to leave the lifestyle I grew up in. There was a recovery ministry inside that church and the pastor was an ex-junky just like me. He was an old school rock and roller who was delivered from a crack cocaine addiction. They used to call him "Hair-Ball." I called him Pastor Mike. He had pictures of himself in a big hair 80's rock band. He was a "been there and done that" kind of person.

I was excited to be a part of what Pastor Mike was doing. I really looked up to him, and I paid close attention to what he did and learned from his ministry. This was something that I wanted to do, and I was dead set on being a part of the ministry. I thought about my family, and the fact that there was no one that we identified with, who knew the Lord. What if there would have been a ministry like this reaching out to my brothers or my mother? What if there had been someone that reached out to me as a young man? There were people there that had tattoos, people who were rough looking, and they were from the same background I was from.

Many of the people that came to the ministry were court ordered; they would even drug test people in the middle of the service. I thought that was cool. To some people this may sound crazy, but to me it was exciting and powerful. You couldn't drag me away from that place. I was not mandated to go there, but I would not be any other place on Thursday or Friday nights. I paid attention and caught on fast. I learned how the pastor set the chairs up, and how he set up the equipment. I would try and get there early and when his car pulled up I would hurry up and help him carry his stuff inside the church.

You might say "sounds like you were sucking up and kissing butt to me." The truth is, I was hungry to learn and wanted what he had; it was worth having. I was willing to do whatever it took to learn all I could from the pastor. My first ministry was carrying the lapel microphone for him and then setting up the chairs. Many times, I talk with folks and hear story after story of how people want to change. Then I ask the million-dollar question, "Are you willing to do whatever it takes?" People say they want to change, but if they are serious then they are willing to do whatever it takes.

The question I mentioned leaves no room for excuses. There must be a 100% commitment. When Jesus said, "Follow me," what if the disciples didn't follow Him? Do you think that He would have waited around for them to make up their minds? Today I owe a debt of gratitude to Pastor Mike, Rev. Jim Snell, and Dewey Huston. Their ministries continue to impact me years later as I sit here in my office writing this book. I think back to that time in my life and I had no clue what God was going to do with me. Being willing to face rejection, ridicule, and be around "normal folks" in the church would be something that I would have to overcome to get there. When you are hungry nothing else matters to you, and I was hungry.

REFLECTIONS AND DISCIPLESHIP:

This chapter is a good lesson of what God can do with someone who has a hunger and thirst for change. I encourage the reader to think about that Scripture in the sermon on the mount. Matthew 5:6 "Blessed are those who hunger and thirst for righteousness, for they shall be satisfied." (ESV) Jesus Himself promised that the person who is hungry for righteousness is the person who will be filled and blessed. Think about the drive a drug addict has that makes them continue their addiction, that drive is intense and unstoppable. That same drive can happen for righteousness.

DISCUSSION QUESTIONS

Use these questions in a small group or discipleship setting. Answer your questions in a notebook following the reading of this chapter.

1. How is your drive for righteousness today? That hunger for spiritual righteousness cannot be produced from man but only from God. Are you willing to stop right now and pray for a hunger and thirst for righteousness?

2. This chapter also touched on a question that is vital to ministry, and recovery alike. That question is the million-dollar question. *Are you willing to do whatever it takes?* What does that look like in your own life?

3. Many accuse me today of being too hard on people in our program. I remember the words of Jesus in Luke 9:52-62. He asks some if they were ready, and they had legitimate excuses like a funeral. He told them they were not fit for the kingdom because they were not willing to do whatever it takes. This is life or death for me, and as serious as if it were terminal cancer. There is no gray area in my life, and I believe that is what it takes. What will it take for you to seek righteousness?

4. I am reminded of the shoe salesman who turned the world upside down. He is most definitely a man

everyone Christian should learn about: D. L. Moody. He heard these words from a preacher and they changed his life. Henry Varley said these words in a prayer meeting: "The world has yet to see what God can do with, and for, and through, and in a man, who is fully and wholly consecrated to Him."[2] Later Moody would hear Charles Hadden Spurgeon preach the good news of Jesus Christ and never be the same again. D.L. Moody was an ordinary man who had one goal in his life, and that goal was to be 100% surrendered to the Lord. That my friends is what it takes. How are you going to demonstrate and live out that you are 100% surrendered to the Lord?

5. God calls us to live our faith and seek righteousness in community (Hebrews 10:25). Who are the people you are going to observe and serve alongside in seeking righteousness?

6. There is a lot about hungering for righteousness in this chapter. How hungry are you now and what are you going to do to fill this hunger?

REFERENCES

1. Wiersbe, W. W. (1996). The Bible exposition commentary. Wheaton, IL: Victor Books.

2. Belmonte, Kevin Charles. D. L. Moody: a Life: Innovator, Evangelist, World-Changer. Moody Publishers, 2014.

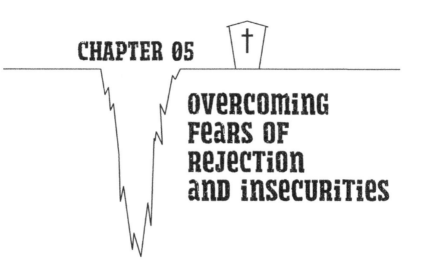

CHAPTER 05

OVERCOMING FEARS OF REJECTION AND INSECURITIES

1 Corinthians 12:26
If one member suffers, all suffer together;
if one member is honored, all rejoice together. (ESV)

Acts 9:26
And when he had come to Jerusalem,
he attempted to join the disciples.
And they were all afraid of him, for they did not believe that he was
a disciple. (ESV)

Imagine a man who was not raised in church and covered in tattoos sitting inside the walls of a church scared and nervous: that was me. I remember wearing turtle neck sweaters during the summer due to the shame of having tattoos on my neck. People would say, "Why are you wearing turtlenecks in the heat of the summer?" I would reply, "I like turtlenecks," even though I only owned one and I wore it all the time.

I remember the fear of rejection I felt walking into the church with all of those "normal people." I am not sure if everyone who comes from a background like mine goes through this, but I know for a fact that many of us do. I would think back on all the wrong that I did, and how much sin I committed. It made me feel so guilty being around all these people who seemed *perfect*.

I am reminded of the Apostle Paul in his letter to the Philippians when he said, "But one thing I do: forgetting what lies behind and straining forward to what lies ahead, I press on toward the goal for the prize of the upward call of God in Christ Jesus." (Philippians 3:13-14, ESV). Paul said he would never forget to look forward and press forward. How could I forget that too? Paul had a rough past, and I believe he might have struggled with the things he had done as well.

I often reflect to the times when I was lost and without Christ growing up. In my family we only went to a church when we were out of food and needed a handout. When I was in the streets in Jefferson City before I went to prison, one time I was in a shelter and I went to church because I had to. I even had a false conversion. I don't remember anyone in my family that was a Christian.

I remember my first church experience as a saved man outside of the prison. I was living in the middle of nowhere in Cuba, Missouri. I was hunting for work and called a van to pick me up from the men's home. As I sat in a cabin in the middle of nowhere waiting on my ride, I kept thinking of how excited I was to attend church as a saved man. I had on my very best clothes, hand me downs and thrift store clothes, but you couldn't tell me that; it was my very best.

I was excited to go and worship the Lord with real "Christians." I was waiting on the porch for the van to come and excited to meet my ride to church. I heard the church bus crunching the gravel as it made its way up the road and to the cabin. You should have seen the look of surprise on the face of the driver of that old church bus when she pulled up. It was a little old lady, and she was not as excited about me going to her church as I was. She was all alone, and I got in the van by myself.

It was just the two of us. As she pulled up, I could almost hear the whistle of an old western showdown and the crackle of tumbleweed blowing across the dusty road. She was afraid of me. In all honestly, I was probably more afraid of her than she was of me. We feared each other. A tattooed ex-convict scared of a little old lady; imagine that. I was more uncomfortable in that van than I was being strip search in Fulton Diagnostic Center in the Missouri Department of Corrections. It was just me, the tatted up ex-con, and the little old lady from Mayberry.

As she drove around picking people up for church, I sat all the way in the back of the bus more uncomfortable than I was in my whole eighteen months in prison. I remember fear coming over me as I walked into that little Baptist church as the people looked at me like "Guard your valuables." I thought, "If there is holy water in this place, someone is going to try and dunk me in it." This was part of my insecurities and knowing what I looked like and where I came from.

The tattoos on my neck, arms, and face that use to make me feel tough, now made me feel ashamed. This church was in the country. It was a place where the population of farm animals were higher than the number of people. There I sat, alone, scared, uncomfortable, when the song leader broke out the hymnals. I knew some of the hymns, we would sing them in the prison church. We sang Victory in Jesus, the Old Rugged Cross, and others. Then in the middle of all that shame and fear it hit me. I thought, "Who's church is this? This church doesn't belong to these people this church belongs to Jesus!"

During the service I found a cross on the wall and thought about what Christ did for me and I began to sing with all my heart -- out of key and everything. In that moment I forgot about the little lady, the holy water, and all my insecurities. I focused on the equality that Christ brings and began to worship. I was having church. I thought to myself, "If these people want to treat me bad because of the way I look, then they are the ones that need to get right with the Lord and not me."

The ride home from church was a lot different than the ride to church. The driver and I talked the whole ride home. She was a sweet woman and she loved hearing my testimony. She happened to be a volunteer at the local jail and visited the inmates often. She peppered me with questions concerning how to minister to the prisoners. Looking back at those times in my early walk I can see the Lord was revealing His plan for my life.

As co-founder of Freeway Ministries, one of my burdens has always been to create a way for people like me to be bridged or meshed into the local church. People from my background have a hard time being around "normal" church folks. Now I understand that we are all messed up and there are no "normal" people. But I did not know that then. It is only by the grace of God that I kept coming to church and stayed plugged in.

Throughout this book you will see that we have planted a total of six outreach ministries in the United States that focus on people with a background like mine. In 2017, we served over twenty-two thousand people attending our Missouri outreaches alone. That does not include what Rick Lechner is doing in the Omaha, Nebraska Freeway Ministries. Freeway Ministries is a place where people can learn to worship, have a hot meal, receive help with clothing, have their children loved on, be introduced to a risen Savior, and be invited into a local church. One of the focuses of the ministry is to introduce people like me into a body of believers through the local church.

I know how it feels to be out of place. I know the terror of sitting in the bus with a little old lady. Right now, you're laughing at me, but I couldn't be more serious. This is one of the reasons I love the concept of Freeway Ministries. We are bridging these two people groups together. At the end of our outreaches we always invite everyone to a local church and will go and pick them up the next day, so they can attend worship at a local congregation. We are passionate to get folks bridged into serving at a Bible believing and preaching church. The point that I want to make is God used this experience to give me a burden to help the next person with overcoming their fears of entering the local church with "normal" church folks.

When you come from a dysfunctional family and everyone around you at a church looks like they are from "Leave it to Beaver," it creates a feeling of being out of place. I know because I have been there. One of my personal ambitions is to help people come together from these two people groups. There is way too much segregation in the church. You have the biker church, the cowboy church, the addict church, the black church, and so on. What about the church being a picture of heaven or Christ's Kingdom?

I am a student of the Bible, and I find no segregation in heaven or in Christ's Kingdom (Galatians 3:28). When I think of the church, I think of the church of Philippi in the book of Acts. The church that I envision is found in Acts 16:11-40. There a rich woman named Lydia and there was a slave girl who was fresh out of demon possession mixed in with an abusive jailer who had been on the edge of suicide.

What I have just described to you is the church of Philippi. Whenever you read the letter to the Philippians in the Bible, you are reading a letter written to those people. That is a wonderful picture of the church and Christ's Kingdom as it truly should be. I know that we can do more if we are together in diversity. How will the ex-junky ever get to know that the business man is not that much different than he is? How will we ever break the barrier down if we do not bridge these people groups together? The Bible is full of what I call "Unity in diversity." This vision has been taking place over six years now, and it is radically changing the dynamics of the local churches all throughout the Midwestern United States.

Today we have three houses currently in Missouri and a location we call "The Ranch." Two Discipleship Houses for women, one for men, and "The Ranch" just outside of Springfield, Missouri in a country town called Marshfield. (Check out the picture at the end of this chapter.) I see the same fear I had on the faces of the people who come into the local churches we partner with. I understand what those people are going through. One of the biggest struggles is recognizing that sometimes judgement goes both ways. We pre-judge them before they get a chance. I tell folks, "Of course they are going to look at you in a different way. There are not too many people who come into the local church covered in tattoos."

There are a few tactful ways to help with this issue. I know that right now someone is going to say, "We are the church, and you cannot put people into groups." That is exactly what I am trying to avoid. I want to see the ex-prostitute and the heroin addict raise her kids in the same childcare as the school teacher who has never seen drugs. I want to see the homeless man join the choir and sing with those who have been in church their whole lives. There are relationships being built and the body of Christ is impacted in ways you cannot imagine.

Let me give you an example. We received a young lady from jail as an alternative to prison. She comes from a very dysfunctional family. Her parents where people who used drugs and she used meth with one of them on a regular basis. She was pimped out from a young age and all she ever knew was drugs and crime. She was in her early twenties. She never had a driver's license, never had a real job, or her own place to live, and church was the last place you would ever see this little girl. She was given to us as one last chance before she went to prison. After a long hard road, she got her life together. She learned how to drive, got her first job, saved her money, got her very own place to live, came to know the Lord, and now she has a church family. She has been discipled now and has a foundation to stand on. I conducted her wedding to a husband who also comes from this same type of background. I walked her down the aisle in front of her drug addict father and handed her off the day of her wedding. I married her to her husband and was honored to be there for this beautiful young woman.

She is a precious little girl who we love dearly. She looks at my wife and I as a mother and father. She has a whole new world of friends. She has people she would have never met if it wasn't for the local church but that is not all. The church also has much to gain from a woman like her as well. They have never seen anything like it. They are learning from this people group. As our people from Freeway Ministries are bridged into the local church and their little kids are growing up together with other kids with parents from different background, lives are being radically changed. The church folks are being educated on the *do's* and *don'ts* of addiction. I can almost hear the chains falling from the generations ahead.

Discipleship Houses, Thanksgiving 2017

DISCIPLESHIP AND REFLECTION

You have read about insecurities and being uncomfortable. We have so many places in the Bible where people are placed in positions that would make anyone extremely uncomfortable. I heard a preacher say one time, "In order to get the fruit you will need to stand on the limb." The Christian walk is not about comfort, and that is a radical thought and radically different than what many have known. How many times in your Christian walk have you seen the blessing of trusting God through being obedient outside of your comfort zone?

Discussion Questions

Use these questions in a small group or discipleship setting. Answer your questions in a notebook following the reading of this chapter.

1. How many Biblical examples can you think of when God placed people in uncomfortable places?

2. Think of the Apostle Paul's conversion. How would you feel if Jesus showed up and told you to go to the leader of ISIS? That is what happened to a man named Ananias. Listen to what Ananias said when Jesus told him that he was to go and pray with the great persecutor of the church. Read Acts 9:13-14 and share your thoughts? Think about that for a minute. The guy with a warrant for your arrest is there to chain you up and do evil things to you, and the Lord wants you to go alone and pray for him. Then after Saul is healed he is placed into a very uncomfortable position. He is sitting at the table with the very people he came to arrest. As a matter of fact, Saul had wreaked havoc on people that they loved recently and now they are eating dinner together. Saul was alone, and you can bet he was placed in a position the was extremely uncomfortable. Once it was all said and done we have thirteen books in the Bible as fruit from Ananias's bravery.

3. How do you think Paul's baptism service went?

4. Think about your discomfort in going to places that you are uncomfortable going. Are you ready to answer the call to go to the uncomfortable places? What are you going to do to prepare yourself?

5. As I sat in the back of the bus on the way to church that first Sunday, and as I rode home, something changed, what was it?

6. There is a lot in this chapter about Christ changing my perspective. What is going to have to happen for you to change your perspective?

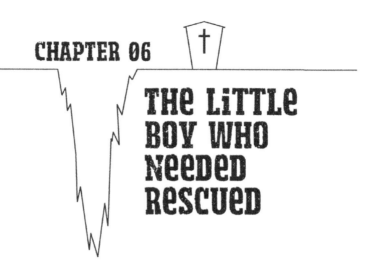

CHAPTER 06

THE LiTTLE BOY WHO NEEDED RESCUED

Psalm 127:3–5

Behold, children are a heritage from the Lord, the fruit of the womb
a reward. Like arrows in the hand of a warrior are the children of
one's youth? Blessed is the man who fills his quiver with them!
He shall not be put to shame when he speaks with his enemies in
the gate. (ESV)

Romans 12:3

For by the grace given to me I say to everyone among you not to
think of himself more highly than he ought to think,
but to think with sober judgment, each according to the measure of
faith that God has assigned. (ESV)

The other day I was spending some time with a new friend I made through our Facebook Live ministry. This new friend of mine and I spent a few hours together before our Springfield North ministry had started. We were sharing life and testimonies with each other when I thought of this leg of my journey. I was thinking back about how all of this went down, and honestly, I don't know how I did it. I know you might be reading this and saying, "You didn't do it, but God did it." That is a correct statement, but I went through it with God. I sometimes wonder if I could do it again.

I shared a Scripture with my new friend that I have buried deep within my heart concerning faith. Romans 12:3 teaches us not to think to highly of ourselves. Our accomplishments are part of the grace of God. Your faith is part of God's gift of grace. I know today that what I am going to share with you is an act of grace. It is a real miracle from God.

I had been preaching for what seemed to be around six months or so at Pastor Mike's outreach ministry when I found out that I was the biological father of a little boy named Keith. I had been with his mother, we will call her Jane, in my past life of drugs and criminality. I will not go into detail of how I met Jane, but it was in the middle of some of my darkest times. We both lived very fast lives. Faithfulness was not a strong point in either of our lives.

I had been very sexually active in the lifestyle I lived, and I had no children. I didn't think that I could have kids due to my lifelong drug abuse. Jane, Keith's mother, was with another guy when she found out she was pregnant, and he had a bunch of kids. Everyone thought this other man was the father. I spent a year in jail and Jane wrote me while in jail. When I got out, I ended up working a construction job and out of a loyalty for Jane writing me, I moved in with her and her mother. She was as big as a house and ready to have Keith at any minute.

I honestly cannot blame Jane for anything that happened because I was just as much at fault as she was. Of course, sin was the cause, and when you live a sinful life it will end in disaster. I was working construction and trying to live the working man's life, but it was like a time bomb was waiting to go off. The foreman was a drug addict I knew from the past. He was a customer of a family member. I would drink when I got off work, on my way home, and when I got home.

When it came time for this little boy to be born, I was there. I remember Jane saying to me "It doesn't matter who the dad is; does it John?" I didn't think he was my son, and no one else did either, including Jane. I refused to sign the birth certificate because I didn't believe he was my son. Looking back, I think I knew deep inside of me he was mine.

I was able to stay out of jail, but the drinking turned to drugging. Jane was drinking, and I was drinking. I ended up leaving, and it wasn't long before the old outlaw was back. It was in prison that I somehow got Jane's address, and I wrote her. My letter was for closure. I wanted to know if

Keith was my son. I asked for a DNA test and she sent me the negative result from the guy who she thought was the father.

The State of Missouri sent someone into the prison to test me to see if Keith was my son. I remember thoughts running through my head. I had no clue how to be a father. I never had one. The men in my life were all outlaws or very dysfunctional people. I didn't know what I would do if he was my son, but I had to know.

It was in that homeless shelter in Springfield, Missouri that I called the Division of Family Services. I asked them to tell me the results. I found out Keith was my son, and I wondered, "How can I possibly be a part of his life? My name isn't even on his birth certificate." I was not married to Jane and I was still fresh out of prison. I was so burdened for this little boy. I knew, at just under two years old he most likely was being drug from one dope house to another or being passed off on anyone who would take him. How could I help this little boy?

I knew he was my responsibility and I had a job to do according to the Word of God (1Timothy 5:8). So, I began to pay child support and pray like crazy. I had no car, no place to live, and a driving record that was everything but pleasant. I had a record of driving without a license, driving while under the influence, and driving with a revoked license. So, there I was a man who rode the city bus to work, cooking at a restaurant with no skills or abilities, and I now had the responsibility to raise a kid. I had no family to help me take care of a kid, and no plan to even take the steps to gain custody. I had no lawyer, no money, and I had no way to travel to see him. But I had faith; I had prayer, and a Bible full of promises toward me.

At the time all this was going on, I was in the early stages of enrolling in Bible College. My heart was so burdened for this little boy who I had not seen with my own eyes since he was a new born baby. His mother called me and told me that she was now homeless with my son and living in motels. I thought, "What are you doing with the $350 a month that I am sending you for child support?" She started sending me pictures of them in motel. I am not sure why she was sending me those pictures. Maybe she thought I would like to see him, but it was ripping my heart out of my chest. I was in a shelter myself, and I had no place that I could take him if she told me I could have him.

I had no interest of being with her, and I definitely was not going back to the area I came from. I was broken and I felt so helpless. I prayed to God for wisdom through this situation, and I had no clue what to do. Then she asked me if I would help her with some money to get into a house. She found a house and was trying to raise the money to move into it. I was selfish, and honestly offended, that she asked me for money. I thought, "How dare her ask me for money to get into a house. What about the money I am already sending her? I am homeless and living in a shelter!"

Then I came under conviction from the Lord. In my heart He whispered to me, "Clean your side of the street John and I will take care of the rest." So, I called her and spoke with her about the situation. I remember it like it was yesterday. I was at the bus stop in front of the Battlefield Mall. I just finished working a twelve-hour split shift and closing the kitchen. I was tired and wet from the closing shift. It was dark, my legs hurt, and the bus was taking forever. I would have to travel through the whole city before I reached my last stop, and then I would walk about a mile to the shelter from there.

It was during that wait for the bus that I had some of the best times meditating and talking with the Lord. I would listen to my MP3 player and worship God while I rode the bus home. It hit me right then to call her. I turned off my music and dialed her number. When she answered I asked her, "How much do you need to get this house?" She told me how much she needed, and honestly, I cannot remember how much it was. I do remember her saying, "Anything will help. How much can you give?" I told her "I am going to pay for all of it, because the Lord told me to clean my side of the street."

You could hear a pin drop on the other side of the phone. The man she was used to was a selfish drug addict who only cared about himself. Then I told her, "I want to tell you something first. The money I am giving to you really belongs to the Lord because I belong to Him. So, you need to be careful what you do with it. If you use this money for the wrong thing, God is going to come down on you." The words she said in reply to me are not appropriate to repeat, but I think you get the point.

I am not sure how much time passed from that time until I received the phone call that would change my life forever. I was cooking in the kitchen of the restaurant that I worked in with the one of the owners, who was now a friend and father figure to me. One of the servers hollered out, "John you have a phone call." That was strange to me, because no one really called me at work. I answered the phone and it was my parole officer, and she sounded panicked. She said, "John your son has just been rescued from a meth lab and the State of Missouri has him in their custody now!" I said "What?" She informed me that I needed to get a hold of them as soon as I could.

I called them and when the lady answered the phone, she was everything but pleasant to talk to. I informed her that I was the father and just found out that this issue had happened to my son. She informed me that the state was going to give custody of this little boy to the family of his biological mother. I knew Jane's family. That would be a nightmare for him. I told her I would fight for him and she snickered at that. She said "Where are you going to take him to? You are living in a homeless shelter and have no car. You have no place to live, and no way to provide for this little boy, Mr. Stroup." I told her in the nicest way possible, "Ma'am I do not know where you stand with Jesus, but He opened this door for me. Jesus can open doors no one can open and shut doors no one can shut. I am going to get my son."

This was one of those Romans 12:3 moments in my life as I look back now. She said, "You have court in less than a week, so I guess we will see you then." She gave me the court date. I worked fifty-five hours a week as a manager and I had no way to get to California, Missouri from Springfield. The weight of the world came down on me and the enemy began to speak those lies into my head. "You are just an old dope addict. How can you possibly do this? You are going to fail this just like you have failed everything else you have ever tried to accomplish." Many people tried to discourage me from going after my son, but that just made me want to do it more. I am a little hard-headed. I tell folks all the time now that they can use their stubbornness for Jesus.

My next struggle was trying to figure out how I would get a ride to court in such a short period of time. It was around two hours one way to get from Springfield, Missouri to California, Missouri. But God placed people in my life like Mona and Leron Wagner. Leron, who was one of the owners of the restaurant I worked for, took me to court that day. As we walked in the court house together I was afraid of what was waiting on the other side of those courtroom doors.

I had seen this child that I was fighting for as an infant and left him for an addiction and the things of this world. His mother and I had a relationship that started in addiction and ended in addiction. I was facing the past and trying to do the right thing for this innocent child that had been through so much. The social worker told me, "Your son is coming up the elevator now." Leron looked at me and I was speechless. I looked at the elevator and watched it get closer and closer to my floor. Then out that elevator came a wild man. He

THE LITTLE BOY WHO NEEDED RESCUED

reminded me of that Scripture concerning Ishmael, "He will be a wild donkey of a man; his hand will be against everyone and everyone's hand against him, and he will live in hostility toward all his brothers" (Genesis 16:12, NIV). This little boy was out of control, no one could get him to settle down, and they even had to take him out of the courtroom for being so loud.

I remember his grandmother having *zero* control over him as he jumped over the benches in the court room. The judge's face was beet-red. Then after the judge asked the bailiff to remove him from the room, the grandmother took him to the hallway, and they shut the door. The judge started to proceed and then the sound of hollering and hitting the walls interrupted the judge once again. This kid sounded like a grown man trying to beat the doors down. I thought. "What have I gotten myself into?" The judge was mad as he looked at this family and said, "Can someone get him under control?" Then Leron looked at me; you could tell he was concerned about my ability to handle this task. I was more afraid than I let on. I was walking by faith without a clue on what was going to happen next. I looked at the team for the state and wondered, "Will they really give this boy to me? This family has been with him, they are not felons, and my record is rough."

Little did I know that those people would one day stand up for me and give that little boy to his daddy. The case worker who oversaw the case had been there from the beginning of Keith being rescued. She was present when the police had raided that meth lab he was in. She was willing to give me the opportunity to prove I was serious about getting Keith and that was all I needed. She invited me to visit with him once a week for small periods of time, and I jumped on it. She told me that I needed a car, a license, and a place to live before I could take him on overnight visits. So I began my journey to rescue my son.

I drove that two-hour trip once a week for five weeks to visit Keith for five minutes, then thirty minutes, then an hour, and then three hours. You get the point. The people who God placed in my life helped me get to see Keith. The old missionary Dewey Huston offered

John and Keith's first visit.

to take me for my first trip. He used his car as a chariot for the Lord. He had brought me to Springfield and now he was taking me to my first supervised visit with Keith.

I did everything that they asked me to do, and the visits increased. I had saved my money while in the shelter. I opened a bank account and didn't spend anything. I was not interested in fancy clothing or a car to drive while in the shelter. I had money put up and was willing to put that money towards getting my son. My first mission was to find a car and God had all that worked out for me as well. Imagine that, right? At the restaurant where I worked, the assistant manager, Becca, and her husband, Joe, were Christians. We developed a strong relationship with each other. Both of them graduated from a local Christian College. God used people like them to assist me all throughout me journey, and He is still doing that today.

I knew a guy whose stepdad owned a car lot.. He said that his dad would sell me a car, and I could pay him in payments. It sounded like a great deal to me. You must understand that I have no clue about cars or anything mechanical. The manager's husband, Joe, was *ear hustling*₁ on our conversation.   He overheard our discussion and approached me later that week. Joe and Becca asked me to come into the office with them. I had no clue what was going on, and they looked so serious. They said, "We overheard your conversation, and the price on that car is way too much. We want to loan you the money to buy a car, and you can pay us back with no interest."

I have an old friend, Dewayne, in Jefferson City who had made it out of the dope and criminal world. Don't get me wrong, he was still very rough. He rode Harleys and was far from Christ-like, but he is still a friend. For some reason I remembered his phone number after all those years away from my home town. I called him and spoke to him. He was and still is a successful business man. I was sharing with him what God is doing in my life and how I was free from drugs and the bondage of addiction. He was happy for me and had always wanted to see me climb out of the gutter. He would try to help me when I was in the pit of addiction, and as you know, no one can help someone who is in active addiction until they are ready for help. He will always be my friend, and he can still be counted on today.

Dwayne and I were talking, and he said "I have this Cadillac that was my wife's car. I will give it to you for $1,500 and you can pay me a little whenever you have it." I had my boss and her husband wanting to loan me the money and my old running buddy wanting to give me a Cadillac on a loan. This is one of those times early in my Christian walk were God was giving me a choice. I could owe my boss or my old running buddy. There are Scriptures clear about debt, partnership, and being yoked to people. One that comes to mind is Proverbs 22:7, "The rich rules over the poor, and the borrower is the slave of the lender."

I chose to be in debt to my boss and borrowed the money from them instead. I love my friend, but the choice to be yoked to Becka and Joe instead was the right choice to make. Now I had a car and could drive to California, Missouri and see my son by myself. This was the kind of thing that God continued to do in my life. This was after almost a year of riding the bus, walking in the rain, getting up in the dark, and journeying through the downtown streets of Springfield early in the morning so that I could make it to work from the homeless shelter.

The case worker, juvenile officer, the lawyer that represented the best interest of the child and even the judge all sided with me. Throughout this book I will speak of the sovereignty of God and the way He has worked in my journey. God used people all through this journey of mine to show me favor. I did everything they asked of me.

I remember going to talk to a landlord for a rental house. His name was Tim. When I went to look at the house, there was literally no floor inside of the home. The roof was horrible looking, but I paid him first and last month's rent in faith. This house happened to be across the street from David's mother-in-law's home. This is the man who was my cellmate in Fulton Prison. If that is not enough to grow your faith, he is also the man who gave me Dewey's address from prison. Now remember my plans were never to move to Springfield, but God's plan was way different than mine. I had the car, I got my license, I got my place to live, and I was taking Keith home for the weekends. It was happening right

in front of my eyes. I was doing what no one thought I could do. I was succeeding at something in my life for the first time. I was going to be a daddy to a little boy, and God was right in the middle of it.

Dewey, Keith, and David's sons at John's first house.

Later I found out that Keith had been taken from his mother twice and he had suffered a fractured skull when he was one. Keith had a limited vocabulary and his favorite word was "No." At the team meeting that was called, the caseworker told the family, "John Stroup is going to take

Keith home today, and that will be the place of residence for him now." They lost it. It was ugly and nasty, but the state was there for me and they had my back. I will never forget that day. I drove home with my son. I couldn't believe that all these people who worked for the state were on my side!

Me! The convicted drug dealer who never did anything right his whole life – the man who was fresh out of prison – was trusted with this little boy. I was a dad now. There were many times that I would walk into that courtroom and those family members would be all lined up behind me in their seats snickering and making little comments. Sometimes I felt outnumbered, but then I remembered the scripture concerning Elisha when his servant thought they were outnumbered and the prophet prayed that God would open his eyes, so he could see who really had the numbers (2 Kings 6:17). I knew that God was with me and I was not alone. I went through those hearings and through the accusations against me from this family to the Department of Family Services. I persevered through all the legal protocols.

I remember being afraid, insecure, and worried about the lies that they would say about me. I remember thinking, "Man these people are going to set me up and get me in some kind of trouble." It was nerve racking. There were even times when I received calls from some of them threatening me. God got me through those times. He showed me that He is faithful. During the whole time of these trials, I kept thinking to myself, "I don't have a car, a house, or a license. How am I going to do all this?" Often when going back to the homeless shelter I would wonder what more I could do to get my little boy out of that bad situation. Then I would say to myself, "No one is going to help him if I don't." It drove me crazy and drove me to pray.

While I was living in that homeless shelter I was saving my money and preparing for my future. This was a period in my life that I can reflect on and be encouraged that the Lord was there strengthening me. Dale Davis in his commentary on 1 Samuel writes, "Sometimes the clearest evidence that God has not deserted you is not that you are successfully past your trial but that you are still on your feet in the middle of it."[2] Looking back at those times I realize that it was the Lord God almighty that kept me going. I get worn out now just thinking about all the things that the Lord accomplished through me during those days. The thing is, I was content with that way of life. I was not complaining, blaming others, or in a hurry to get out of the shelter that I lived in. I was not looking for a car nor did I have a desire to have one before I needed one to see Keith. In my opinion, that is, why God blessed me. I was seeking Him first and not things of this world (Matthew 6:33).

My lawyer was paid by the State because the case was a criminal case due to the charges on Keith's mother for endangering him and his little sister. His name was Van Adams. Once the case dealing with endangerment ended Van was no longer a free lawyer and I had no money to pay Van or any other lawyer. Van happened to be the lawyer that had won a custody case against Keith's birthmother. He knew

Keith's family well. He told me "The state will not pay me for a civil case John, and I cannot represent you for free on this." Van was a rough fella who smoked cigarettes and had a loud booming voice. I remember him saying "John you need to talk to your people and see what they can come up with to help you. Once the judgment is made it will be over, and there is not a civil order for custody." I had no clue what amount was going to be to afford an attorney, but I knew it had to be in the thousands of dollars. It might as well had been three million dollars; I knew I didn't have that kind of money for sure. I knew that I had to have it though, so I prayed and cried out to the Lord. It was all I could do.

During the trial I got to know Mr. Van, and through sharing with him, we developed a friendship. When that criminal case was almost over he said, "John I had my doubts about you when we first met. After spending this time with you and getting to know you, I believe you are the real deal. I am going to represent you pro-bono (for free). Just fill out this paperwork for me and we will start your civil case for the custody of your son." In custody proceedings like this one, once the state closes their case, anyone could take Keith from me, because there was no ruling on his custody. So, the state and my lawyer worked together to protect Keith. They made sure no one could take him.

For once in my life, the law was on my side. I am reminded of the verse in Proverbs concerning the Lord giving favor through authority. "The king's heart is a stream of water in the hand of the LORD; He turns it wherever He will"

(Proverbs 21:1, ESV). They kept the case open for the next year while I fought for custody of Keith. Imagine the shock that I felt when the weight of this situation finally hit me. I got a free lawyer, the state on my side, and I was going to be a single father. I was just living in a homeless shelter, I had just got out of prison, and I was still on parole for selling drugs in a school zone, but I had a fighting chance to get my son.

While Keith's birth mother was in prison, I got full custody of this two year old little boy. Before the trial ended the juvenile lawyer that represented the best interest of Keith said, "I want it on the record that it is in the best interest of this child to remain with his father." When those words came out of that attorney's mouth I thought back from the first time I walked through those courtroom doors. I had many doubts about what God was going to do. What were the chances I had to really get this little boy? I was a man that had done nothing but fail his whole life. I had been out of prison for less than a year. I had no family around, but I wanted my son and needed to do what God had put on my heart to accomplish.

That first day when I stood in front of those courtroom doors, I had no clue about the stress and struggles that were ahead of me. That first day in court everyone thought that Keith's mother's family was going to get guardianship of Keith and his younger half-sister. Then I walked through the door; the judge stopped the guardianship right then. They were so mad, angry, and upset they couldn't even talk. Then my day had arrived, and I walked out of that court with those papers in my hand.

I still have those papers today that say, "sole custody". God did that for me, and it is a miracle that reminds me that God is with me. I feel like Joshua the great leader of the Israelite army when the Lord took him back to the place where he once failed as a leader and said "Have I not commanded you? Be strong and courageous. Do not be afraid; do not be discouraged, for the LORD your God will be with you wherever you go" (Joshua 1:9, NIV). I cannot help but think of the Ark of the Covenant in the Old Testament when it comes to these times in my life. Inside the Ark of the Covenant were items that reminded the Israelites of times and places when God showed up. They were times when they could not help themselves. They were reminders of God providing for them in a miraculous way.

The Ark housed manna from heaven, Aaron's rod that budded, and pieces of the Ten Commandments. For me, the papers that say *sole custody* and that prison Bible I read so much that it split in two are both inside my Ark of the Covenant. They are reminders of when God showed up and did things when I was helpless to do anything for myself. Please take note for yourself of times when the Lord showed up and keep things to remind you of the fact that the Lord is with you. I share these things with my kids, guests that come to my home, and at events where I speak.

I want to encourage you, if you are reading this and struggling, think of those times when God showed up and showed off in your life. Think of those times and reflect on them. Do not forget those moments and keep reminders of them. Share those moments with people God puts in your life. If you are reading this and you have never experienced the saving grace of God, do it now. Accept the fact that you are a sinner who was born shaking his fist at God. Ask the Lord to forgive you and respond to His precious sacrifice on the cross. I encourage you to read the Bible and ask God for faith to understand His Word. If God can do this with my life, He can do it for anyone.

My journey had begun. I was a single father of a damaged little boy. He was still in diapers and only God knows what all he had been through. I wondered about sexual abuse, mental issues, as well as health problems due to the things that he had been through in such a short amount of time. I had no clue what I was doing, but I knew it was the right thing. So, I rolled with the punches. This is one of many places in my walk with the Lord that taught me to depend on Him. I truly believe that God tests us like He did the men and women all throughout the Bible.

I think of Abraham and how God called him from everything he had ever known unto a brand-new life. Abraham was a lost man and living in a culture of idolatry (See Genesis 12). Old Abe was called away from that place, and left where he was from, not knowing where he was going. God put a down payment of righteousness on his account (Romans 4:22-24). The Scripture says that Abraham is the father of all those who follow in the same pattern of faith (Romans 4:16). "[Abraham] did not waver through unbelief regarding the promise of God, but was strengthened in his faith and gave glory to God" (Romans 4:20, NIV). This is a perfect picture of what the Lord has done in my life. God has put things in front of me, from the prison cell to the pulpit, time and time again. I look back and see how God promoted me to a new level of faith through those times when things seemed impossible.

This book is written to encourage the reader that all things are possible with God! Even things that are impossible with man (See Matt 19:26). How can a man like me become a successful single father? How can someone whose main objective in life was to stay as high as he could, become the director of a non-profit ministry? How could I raise this little boy with all this baggage and no parenting skills whatsoever? I never took a parenting class. Shoot, there is not a text book, program, seminar, or a rehab that could have helped a man like me! Warren Wiersbe put it best "The dead do not need resuscitation, the dead need resurrection."[3] God did it, He raised me from the dead. He alone gets all the glory. To God be the glory!

So, there I was a man, with a two-year-old little boy, and the only words that I could remember him saying repeatedly was "No." I remember the conversations with him. "Keith do you want to go have ice cream?" "No." He would say. "Keith do you want to go and play?" "No." "Keith do you love your dad?" "No." It was a nightmare.

He was in diapers and I had very little experience changing a diaper. To this day I know that one of the greatest miracles that God did on my journey from the pit to the pulpit was helping me potty-train my son. One day Keith and I were at church and I noticed him grabbing his private part. I thought, "Oh no, I forgot to put a diaper on him! He is going to pee his pants!" I had a van full of homeless folks to drop off. I grabbed him like a fumbled football and ran with him like I was going to score a touchdown in the fourth quarter. I was on a mad dash to the restroom. I discovered he didn't want to pee in his pants. I thought, "That is brilliant, I will just keep his diaper off and wait until he has to pee!" It worked out, and that is pretty much the way I learned how to parent. Trial and error often guided my decisions.

The Lord was busy helping me for sure. I guarantee that the Lord encamped His angels around me during that part of the journey (Psalms 34:7). I remember trying to do things like take a shower, get dressed, and make breakfast with this little terrorist running around the house. I had so many fears that I was going to fail, or something was going to happen to him. I remember one day I left him in the car setting in the driveway feet from the back door for just a second and he somehow got out of his seat. He was behind the wheel about to crash the car into the back of the house. I remember the first night I woke up to hear him coughing. He sounded like a seal on the discovery channel, so I rushed him to the hospital to find that he had a respiratory issue called the croup.

There were many times being so tired from staying up all night that I could hardly hold my head up from working ten hours in the kitchen at the restaurant. There were times when I could barely pay my day care bill, and through all that we made it. Keith and I survived potty training, the terrible threes, the biting, the daycare fees, the single parenting, the learning how to talk, and finally saying something besides "No!"

As I write this book Keith will be eleven-years-old. He is healthy, he loves Jesus, he has never seen drugs, alcohol, heard a curse word from his father's lips, and he has been in church every time the doors are open since the day I brought him home. He now has a family that loves him, and I have committed to protect and care for him with all I have until the Lord calls me home. My wife is good mother, and Keith is being raised in a Christian family. I struggle with being a godly father, and to be honest, being a father is probably one of the hardest things I have ever had to do, but it is worth it. I never had a dad, but, by the grace of God, my son does. This is a blessing from the Lord, and according to the Bible children are a gift given by the Lord (Psalms 127:2-3).

I feel honored and humbled that the Lord would allow me the chance to have a family and trust me enough to raise children. You will read later that God showed me more favor by allowing me to have a wife who had two children of her own. Through all the struggles God has blessed me repeatedly as I walk by faith.

DISCIPLESHIP AND REFLECTION

This chapter discusses how Keith needed to be rescued. It also discussed the sacrifices that were made to ensure Keith's protection and custody. In many ways this is the picture of salvation. Jesus Christ came to save those who could not save themselves. Jesus Christ sacrificed Himself and lived selflessly to save a lost world. This changes one's identity from a dead orphan to a new creation (2 Corinthians 5:7). That should make one not only want to accept the gift of Jesus (Ephesians 2:8-9) but acknowledge that it was a work God.

DiSCUSSiON QUESTiONS:

Use these questions in a small group or discipleship setting. Answer your questions in a notebook following the reading of this chapter.

1. Think back to the fact that Keith needed rescued. Was there ever a time in your life where you needed rescue, and someone stepped in to save you?

2. There are people from your past that might need rescued themselves. How will you go about making sure to communicate the hope found in Christ while at the same time remaining steadfast in your commitment to a new life?

3. In this chapter John talked about how he had always been the one who failed, but something changed inside of him. How will you deal with your past and getting beyond your failures from the past to show that you have been raised from death to life?

4. There are many examples in this chapter of times when John had to demonstrate that he was not the "old John." What are some objective steps you will have to take to demonstrate that you truly are committed to Christ?

5. John had to learn many new things. These new things were not easy. What are you expecting to have to change to be the person God has called you to be?

6. In this chapter John discussed how some people witnessed the change in his life take place over time. Who are some people that you will have to spend time demonstrating with evidence the change that has taken place in your life?

References

1. *Ear hustling* is when you eavesdrop.
2. Dale Davis.
3. Wiersbe, W. W. (1996). The Bible exposition commentary (Vol. 1, p. 531). Wheaton, IL: Victor Books.

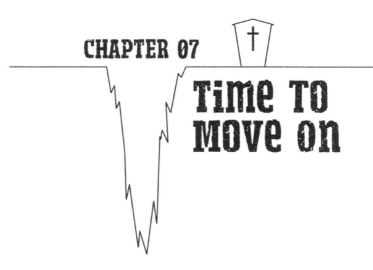

CHAPTER 07

TIME TO MOVE ON

Galatians 1:10

For am I now seeking the approval of man, or of God?
Or am I trying to please man? If I were still trying to please man, I
would not be a servant of Christ. (ESV)

Acts 5:29

But Peter and the apostles answered, "We must obey God rather
than men. (ESV)

There were many times in my journey where I had to continue to lean on God's understanding. This is another season of my walk where once again my faith was tested, and it was a time when my faith was deepened. I remember the pain that this stage in my life caused for me and many others. I want to let you in on the fact that many times when you are in a stage of growth with the Lord there will be many who will not agree with what you are doing. This part of my journey separated me from most of the men that I looked up to and things were never the same again. I had been in the same church for around a year and I was very plugged into the ministry there. I was preaching, teaching, and I was an active part of the men's ministry.

I began to come under conviction from God concerning doctrinal issues. When I came to know the Lord, I didn't have a clue the differences between Baptist, Pentecostal, Catholic, Methodist, or any other denominational group. The Lord protected me from getting swept away by the wrong group. I disagreed strongly with some of the beliefs of the church I was in. I also disagreed with some of the theological beliefs of Dewy as well. Please understand that I mean no harm by what I am saying. I hope everyone figures out what they believe the Gospel is clear on and they are sure of where they stand on those fundamental truths. I loved those people and still do, but I could not continue to follow a pastor and be a part of a church when I disagreed with what they taught. I would have grown bitter and become a fake if I did that. I thought to myself, "Where am I going to go?" I was preaching at this church. Folks were being saved and people were coming to the church. My son was making friends and the people accepted me. But the conviction of the Lord would still not leave me alone.

I thought about Dewey and how much this would hurt him and his wife if I left. They became like a family to me and we were very close. My son called him "Papa Dewey." I knew that it would crush him, but the pressure to leave was so strong from the Lord. I had started a ministry picking up the homeless men from the shelter and the impact of leaving this ministry weighed heavy on me. Thinking back to that time it reminds me of when the Lord wouldn't allow Paul to preach in Asia and held him back (Acts 16:5-7). It sounded so crazy, but it was the Lord preventing me from leaving.

The Lord protects us in His sovereign plans. During my stay in prison I desperately wanted to learn the Bible in and out. I thought that Dewey was the one that the Lord sent to teach me the Bible but looking back I was wrong about that. Even though Dewey made the largest impact on my Christian walk, it became clear that Dewey was sent into my life for something else. God sent Dewey to show me how to love people like Christ.

While in prison I had neighbor that lived across the cellblock from me named "Rudy". He had been in the same cell for twelve years and had five more to serve before he could be released. Rudy noticed that I was different from the rest of the men. He saw that I was a Christian. Rudy was also a believer and he became a dear brother in Christ to me. He started bringing me these papers that he acquired somehow from the chaplain's library and they turned out to be commentaries on the Bible. I had never heard of such a thing as a commentary before that, but they were an answer to my prayers. Verse by verse my journey began dissecting and searching for the truth of God's Word.

There were all kinds of different commentaries, but there was a certain one written in a way that intrigued my heart. I would go through a new stack every so often and dig out the ones that were written by a man named Warren Wiersbe. I never knew who the person was who wrote those commentaries, because they were copied from the chaplain's library and the author never mentioned his name. These resources were more valuable than gold. I could sit down with my Bible and many of my questions would be answered through diligent study of the commentary. Verse by verse I would take notes, it was as if the author was speaking to me. I was learning and hungry to learn. I wrote his name down and committed to reading more of what he wrote after my release from prison.

During this time of wrestling with doctrine, I heard about a group of men who were meeting in a coffee shop on Wednesday nights. These guys were from all different backgrounds and churches. I almost didn't go. The first night I met two gentleman, Mike Aye and Rick Lechner. Mike Aye was an delivery driver and Rick was an ex-con who oversaw a trucking company. These men would become the other two co-founders of Freeway Ministries and serve as best men in my wedding.

This was the beginning of something that would change all our lives and the lives of countless others. Little did we know that this was the beginning of Freeway Ministries.

Mike Aye was a struggling Christian who had an addiction to pornography that almost destroyed his marriage. Mike had what I thought was the perfect family; a great wife, two beautiful kids, and a nice home.

I got to know Mike well and he became a part of my family. Mike and his family were what we call church hoppers; they were never in church for much length of time, and that gave me the opportunity to invite them to come to the church I was involved with. Mike, Julie, Kolby, and Macy accepted my invitation to check out my church. The Aye family started coming to the ministry, and they treated me and my son like one of their own. Mike and I talked on the phone on a regular basis and prayed together regularly.

I would make fun of Rick for being Baptist. I called him Baptist Rick. I didn't know the difference between a Baptist and a hole in the ground. I was Baptist in doctrine and didn't even know it. Rick and I had a lot in common. We were just alike, and it felt like God was giving me another chance to have a family. Rick had a family of six and a wife who was just as rough as he was. When it boils down to it, she is probably tougher then him. We all became very close.

Our little coffee shop Bible study got big. People began to hear about it and come from all over the place to be a part of it. Mike Aye had the key to the coffee shop and we would have the parking lot full of cars. People started getting saved, lives began to change, and the Lord was doing a work that could not be explained by men. Rick and Mike began to come to the church that I was a part of for the ministry event on Friday's. They were a part of my family now, and we were developing a bond that would change all our lives.

I was preaching at the soup kitchen and the shelter on a regular basis. Rick and Mike would go with me most of the time. God was doing such a work in all our lives. What started off as a little Bible study in a coffee shop, from people that were so different from each other, would become Freeway Ministries. We had one thing in common though. We were all hungry for the Lord, and all of us were once lost and on our way to hell until Jesus saved us. None of us would have hung out together if it were not for the common bond that held us together; and His name is Jesus.

I had made my decision to leave the church that I attended. I had been in that church for around a year, and almost everyone accepted me. My son was used to the environment. Dewey and his wife were there as well. I was picking people up every week and bringing them to church from the shelters and the streets. Why would I leave? I was preaching two and sometimes three times a month. People were being saved. I loved my Sunday school class and I knew many of the people who went to the church.

I felt like I was betraying Dewey Huston, and his wife Connie, by leaving. There was a sense of betrayal as well toward the pastor that gave me the chance to preach in his outreach ministry. I had no clue where I was going to go; honestly, I was afraid. I set up a meeting with the pastor of the church and expressed my disagreement on doctrinal issues. I told him that I was grateful for him preaching and teaching me the Word for the time I had been there. I shared that I was having a hard time due to the interruptions from what they called a "gift of the Spirit." See there was a lady who would interrupt the service repeatedly with this so-called gift that was anything but Biblical from my convictions.

It was like the Lord was saying "get out now." The pastor must have thought, "Who does this guy think he is?" I was just released from prison and fresh out of a homeless shelter sitting in a Pastor's office telling him I disagreed with his doctrine. I had to do what God was leading me to do, and I could not be fake. I gave a two-month notice to the men's ministry and to the outreach ministry I was involved in as well. I told the pastor of the recovery ministry I would preach for him as much as he needed. God was in the middle of this and I didn't know it yet. Now let me make something crystal clear. I love my brothers who are Pentecostal. God used a Pentecostal man to make the single largest impact on my life. With that being said, I disagree with some of the doctrine of the Pentecostal church.

Dewey showed me how to love like Jesus! For that I am grateful. To this day I have not seen anyone have that same kind of love as Dewey did. I left the office of this pastor on a Sunday morning telling him my disagreements. I felt insecure and under qualified. This pastor was a professor at a local Bible college and I was an ex-con with a G.E.D. and no college. You may think "Why the meeting then?" The reason I met with the pastor was because I respected him enough to let him know why I was not going to be there anymore. I did not want him to think that those seats were empty due to something he did or him have to wonder what happened.

Please allow this leg of my journey be a lesson for you. If you are struggling with a doctrinal issue from the church, please talk to the pastor. Do not just leave the church. Pray about it and then talk to the leadership out of love. I know what kind of church I was in and I understand what they believe. I would not expect a church to change the way they operate for me, but I cannot go against my God given convictions either.

The same Sunday I left the church I preached that night at the Salvation Army Shelter I used to live in. I went there around 5:00 p.m. and Rick was with me. He met me there, and we prayed together at an altar. We prayed that God would open the door for a ministry that would reach the people group that we were after. We desperately wanted to start our own recovery ministry. Rick went to a Baptist Church that I had never attended but his church planned one day to have a recovery ministry. The church was in the middle of a building program and had at least a year until it was going to finish the building.

I still remember the prayer I said that night at the Salvation Army. We prayed that the Lord would open the doors for a ministry that we wanted to start. That night I thought nothing of that prayer, but the next day I sure did. Rick called me the next day and I could hardly understand him due to his excitement. He said, "John you are never going to believe this! My pastor called me and told me to draw up the plans for a recovery ministry" That next Wednesday I was in Pastor Eddie Bumpers office discussing our ministry. God showed me He was in control. I never missed a church service throughout the times I left the other church. Even though I had no church to go to, the Lord did not allow me to miss one service. He has a plan and we must step out in faith.

I remember looking across the room at this pastor that was talking with a strong southern accent. He was feeling me out and I could see the look on his face, "Who is this guy, and is he for real?" I didn't know what to think of this Baptist preacher. I had never met a Baptist pastor before. I had no clue what to expect in the service or how they worshiped the Lord. I told him I would preach at any church that I was asked to preach in. I also shared my heart with him as he did with me. I told him that the people we were going to reach were not your average church folks and that they didn't know any of the church rules. I told him that they would stir up his church member's and he said, "They may need to be stirred up."

I told him that some may break into the building, smoke in front of the doors, and even wear a hat in the sanctuary. He said, "Bring it on." This was a very conservative Southern Baptist Church. He hollered out into the room where the secretary was and said, "Make sure that no one uses those vans on Saturday's." Then he looked over across the yard and pointed at this little house that was behind the church and said, "You can use that building across the property, and if there comes a day that you outgrow that building, we will see about putting you in another building."

The first night we had Freeway Ministries, we had worked hard for more than a month. We prayed, fasted, handed out flyers, and ended up with a paper that had seven names on a list for the vans to pick up. I remember thinking, "What if no one shows up?" I had been preaching to a large group in my last church. There was so much fruit from that ministry and then I left with nowhere to go. There I sat with seven people on a list looking at those names and wondering if I had made a mistake. My co-laborers had the same look on their faces. None of us had a degree, or were educated, and quite frankly had no clue what we were doing. We knew Jesus though. It was the Lord that would make this work a success, not men.

We decided to search for chairs throughout the property and put up every chair that we could find. We found almost fifty chairs. Every chair was filled, there were people everywhere in that little house, and God moved on us. It was one of the many things that the Lord did in my life that I will never forget. How do you think that the pastor felt when he received that phone call? "Hey pastor, we outgrew our building the first night." This was the start of Freeway Ministries.

We would move to the church gym only to outgrow the gym. Then finally we moved into a permanent gym that would be our meeting place for the next six years. We had no clue what to expect. We had no idea the work that God was about to do through a bunch of rag-tag fellas. God knew what He was going to do, all we had to do was trust Him. I had people try and tell me what a mistake I was making. I will never forget the call that I received from a deacon's wife. She said, "John, if you do not receive the baptism of the Holy Spirit with the evidence of tongues you will spend your Christian walk driving without power steering fluid." I still have not experienced anything like she was talking about, but I can tell you that I have seen the power of God repeatedly.

I can also say that people are always going to disagree with you when you are doing what God has called you to do. Follow your God-given convictions, test them against Scripture, and do it anyway. If you don't, then you will live the rest of your life regretting it. Even though leaving that church was one of the hardest things that I have ever done, it is probably one of the most important things I have ever done. Boy did we have some work to do.

Dewey Huston's prison letters and addresses collected after his death. We release a monthly newsletter to prisoners called The Dewey.

Rick, John, and Mike: the founders of Freeway Ministries.

Mike, John and Rick at John's wedding.

Discipleship and Reflection

This chapter demonstrates the difficulty of trusting your spiritual convictions and discernment despite the advice of others. It also demonstrates how vital it is to understand doctrinal issues. God puts people in your life sometimes only for season and only to accomplish a certain task. We don't always know what that task is, but God will reveal this to us later. Most importantly, one observes that walking in faith requires a devotion to God's word and acting upon the clear teaching of Scripture.

Discussion Questions:

Use these questions in a small group or discipleship setting. Answer your questions in a notebook following the reading of this chapter.

1. What will you do in the future to test your convictions against God's Word?

2. Have you begun to recognize individuals who have served a purpose in directing your walk in faith? What are some of the common attributes you have identified in these individuals?

3. John spoke about a difficult conversation with his former pastor. Have you ever had a similar discussion? What was it like?

4. Sometimes individuals who love the Lord must part ways (Acts 15: 36-41). In the future you may have to part ways with other believers. How will you prepare yourself now for some of those difficult conversation? What can you do to make sure that your departure from other Christians will be handled in a way that glorifies God?

5. There is a time for everything under the heavens (Ecclesiastes 3:1–8). In your life, how will you know when it is a time for you to move on?

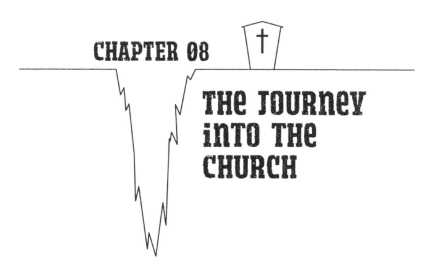

CHAPTER 08

THE JOURNEY INTO THE CHURCH

Hebrews 10:25

not neglecting together, as is the habit of some, but encouraging one another, and all the more as the Day drawing near. (ESV)

Acts 4:13

Now when they saw the boldness of Peter and John, and perceived that they were uneducated, common men, they were astonished. And they recognized that they had been with Jesus. (ESV)

Having read the verse above from Acts 4:13, I think often on the look that Peter and John received from the religious crowd that day as they boldly preached the things pertaining to the risen Savior. The Bible teaches us that the

Pharisee's were astonished, or marveled at these uneducated, and common men. I asked myself "what makes a Pharisee marvel?" and "How did their faces look as they proclaimed God's Word in power with boldness?" I think the same way many of the Baptist church members looked as us as we drove a big purple van into the parking lot of a conservative Baptist church that said "Ozark Assemblies of God" on it. There I was, a convicted crack dealer, on parole, a single father, and driving an old purple church van that read "Ozark Assembly of God" in big gold letters into a traditional Southern Baptist Church. I'm covered in tattoos all over my neck and face. The goal for Freeway Ministries is to create a bridge into the church for people with absolutely no church background. That was my heart, and it is one of the goals of the other founders and I have shared from day one. This was not going to be easy, and many of the church members gave me a look that reminded me of that little old lady who first picked me up from church in Steeleville, Missouri.

God was going to turn that Baptist church upside down. As Dick Templeton says, "Freeway Ministries caught me by surprise, and I was not ready for it." Dick has been a member of the church for over thirty years. God used Freeway Ministries to change the dynamics of the church and those who were in it. I had no clue what it meant to be Baptist, but that was okay. God knew what He was doing.

We started going after people from the streets and hunting down Rick Lechner's old friends that he used to use drugs with in his wilder days. That Bible study that Mike Aye started in that little coffee shop transitioned into that little white house behind the church were we first started Freeway Ministries. At first, no one knew what to think of the people that we were bringing into the church. Through it all, a big change began to happen. The bridging of the ministry into the church became an act of God.

Paul, the pastor over missions and discipleship, was a huge part of this all. He was on our side and all for what God was doing through the local church. He was excited to see the church being so missional in its own back yard. I remember when Rick Lechner called me to go and visit with one of his old friends who was using and selling drugs. His name was Mike. Rick said, "I want you to come with me to the trap house Mike is staying at." I had no clue what I was walking into. Knowing that trap houses are for one thing, and that is selling drugs, and getting high.

A trap house is a very dangerous place. The guy we were going to see, Mike, was also very dangerous. He had lost a son and was hurting so bad that he didn't care if he lived or died. Rick and I drove the purple van I owned over there and went to talk with him. Honestly, I was hoping that no one was home. I was still on parole and headed to the trap house to share Christ.

There were others with us in the van but no one else went to the door but Rick and myself. We knocked, and no one answered the door. Once everyone in the van knew that it was safe they exited the van and gathered around the yard with us to pray for God to intervene on this man's life. We asked the Lord to enter this place of brokenness and do whatever it took to get Mike to a place of surrender.

Not too long after we left, Mike came home and reviewed the camera footage. He saw his old friend Rick and some fella covered in tattoos who drove a purple church van praying in his yard. You can imagine his surprise. He was not a happy camper and he thought I was a cop. Days later Mike was in a highspeed chase with the police and almost died. In the jail cell he cried out to the Lord and asked the Lord to send a man to be a father to his little girl. He was bonded out and started coming to Freeway Ministries.

He got involved in the local church right away. Mike became the head of our security for years and God did mighty things through his testimony. Mike's fight is not over yet, but we continue to do what we can to help him and many others through the simplicity of the Gospel. This is the mission of Freeway Ministries. We are watching people like Mike be radically changed. These are the types of people that we are trying to reach. This is the plan we have.

If we can get them out of the trap house and into the church house, then we have accomplished something through our ministry. What better missionaries are there to reach this people group than the ones who have been delivered from the lifestyle? Mike had a brother we would try and reach on a regular basis. We would stop by his house, and he would hide from us like I used to hide from the police when they came knocking on the door.

One day we stopped by Mike's brother's house and no one would answer the door. As we walked away a short, chubby fella came running out of the house trying to make it to his car. Rick chased after him, and he caught him in the driveway. It was Mike's cousin, Barry. Barry was the one we wanted to go away. We saw Barry as the bad influence on Rick's old friends. Rick said, "They would be a lot better off if that Barry would stop coming around! He is the one giving them the dope." Barry was the one that we thought would continue to bring drugs around and drag the others down. We had no clue what God was doing through this situation.

Now don't get me wrong -- Rick never stopped trying to reach any of his old friends; he didn't give up on people. Springfield, Missouri is where Rick is from, he had a history with these people, not me. That would soon change in a big way. The guy we were after to this day is still avoiding us and promising to come, but Barry is another story. Today Barry is six years sober, has a good job as an electrician, he's married, and he plays a big part in the lives of all his kids. He is a vital part of a local partnering church and is a leader on the security team at Freeway Ministries. You may wonder how this all happened.

Barry had a girlfriend who worked for the State of Missouri. She had a clean background, a nice home, a clean ride, good credit, and everything a drug dealer looks for in a woman. She would hide Barry out and rent him cars to drive. One night, the police kicked in her door when they were after Barry, and they took her and Barry to jail. She lost her daughter, her job, and spent all her money getting Barry bounded out of jail. Barry left her shortly after he was arrested and came back high on meth. She told him, "I don't want you to be one of those people that I have to leave behind. I am through with this life."

Barry woke up to the reality that she cared about him, and he was about to lose her. He showed up at Rick's house at the midnight hour banging on the door. When you are in a ministry like ours, there is no telling what could be waiting on the other side of the door in the middle of the night. Rick answered, and it was the last person he expected to be; it was Barry high as a kite. He was with his girlfriend who I am pretty sure was drunk at the time.

Rick asked Barry what he wanted, and Barry said, "We need help. What do we need to do?" Rick told Barry the most spiritual thing you can think of. "I can't help you!" Now if you know Rick this will bring a smile to your face. Rick knows that only Jesus can help a person like Barry. Rick went way out of his way to give Barry and Heather a hand. Barry couldn't go to treatment because of how high his blood pressure was. That is what happens when your high on meth, overweight, and paranoid of the police. Heather entered a local treatment center, and Barry got kicked out of one for cursing the staff out (he later apologized).

Barry came to our new Bible study we had started. Barry was nervous, out of place, but he was there and that is what mattered. He was hurting and needed the compassion that the Body of Christ brings. When I tell you, he had no clue about the things of God I mean he really had no clue. He walked in with the prison strut. Some of you know what I am talking about. He looked at all of our Bibles and said, "Cool, everyone has a different looking Bible. Kind of like everyone has a different kind of pistol huh?" Then he said, "Man, I want one of those!"

After we all settled into the study, it was clear that Barry was broken. I was sharing Psalms 51 with him and right there in that Bible study Barry gave his heart to the Lord. It wasn't a fancy prayer, but it was a simple child-like prayer to God. What happened next cannot be made up. We walked across the parking lot to the church for a prayer meeting. This was Barry's very first church service. He had just got off the phone with his girlfriend, Heather, who was in treatment. He told her that they could not be together intimately anymore because he was a Christian. She thought he had lost his mind, and she was not ready for the new Barry.

We entered the church for service and Barry was a nervous wreck. If he felt out of place before, he really felt out of place now. We ended up on the stage on our knees for prayer. After the microphone was passed around for people to pray, Barry asked a question that left us almost out of breath from laughing at him. He said "Hey, guys what religion are we anyway?" He was serious as a heart attack! The more we laughed the more Barry got upset. Barry was like "Why are you guys laughing at me? What religion are we?" Now mind you, we are standing in the middle of a Baptist church sanctuary, and we just got finished with a prayer meeting. What Barry really meant to ask was "What denomination are we?"

My point is that Barry was raw, fresh, unchurched, and simple. Today Barry and Heather are married. They are raising their kids in the church house and not the dope house. Barry went to trial, and they gave him probation even though he should have gone to prison.

Barry, Heather, and their kids, living for the Lord.

The judge knew that Barry was a changed man. Barry never had a job before and he was pushing forty-years old. Today Barry is working for a good company and learning to be an electrician. You never know what God is going to do, and you should never count anyone out. Too many times we assume that we know what will happen to a person or who will be used of God. Many times, we are wrong, and honestly, it is sinful to take this approach to our Christian walk.

Heather gave her life to Jesus as well. They serve in the local church and are both vital to our ministry. Barry got custody of his daughter. He is not on probation anymore, and he loves Jesus as much or more than anyone I know. I had the privilege of working with Barry through discipleship. Barry has been changed and no one can deny it. He is now a member of the local church and the church folks see that it is possible for someone like Barry to be changed by the Gospel.

Barry's kids are being raised in the church with the kids of police officers from our community. This is what it is all about friends, and it is a big reason we do what we do.

If Freeway Ministries would not focus on planting ministries alongside local churches we would be deemed a "drug church" or an "addict church," and the two people groups would never be blended or meshed together. Barry and a captain of the Sheriff's department are now friends. How is that for a miracle? The same guy who has slapped cuffs on Barry now shakes his hand and serves alongside him in the same church. Their kids go to the same Sunday school class together! Friends, this is how we make an impact on our community.

REFLECTIONS AND DISCIPLESHIP

God is in the business of changing people (Ephesians 2:1-5). This chapter has focused on how God has not only used Freeway Ministries to change people but, to change His church. God also pursues the lost (Luke 19:10). Freeway Ministries has committed itself to be a ministry that is the means God uses to seek out those who have often found themselves on the outskirts of society and the church. Isn't it encouraging to know that God uses people who are committed to seeking the lost to find them.

DISCUSSION QUESTIONS

Use these questions in a small group or discipleship setting. Answer your questions in a notebook following the reading of this chapter.

1. In this chapter there are numerous examples of God putting people in the right place, at the right time, to act as the means through which individuals are brought to salvation. Of the stories in this chapter, which one speaks most directly to you?

2. The author noted that Rick does not give up on people. Who have been the people in your life that did not give up on you?

3. Who are the people in your life that you cannot give up on? Take a moment now to pray for those people that God might put you in the right place, at the right time, to speak the truth of the Gospel into their lives.

4. When Barry first entered the church and came to salvation there were many things he did not know. As you grow in your faith, how can you help individuals like Barry who knew nothing about "the truth that was once for all delivered to the saints?"

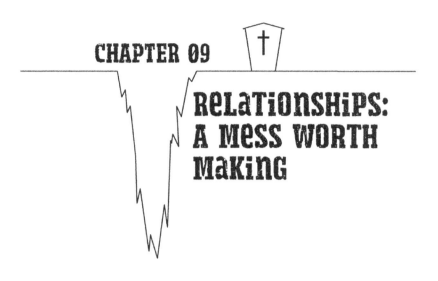

CHAPTER 09

RELATIONSHIPS: A MESS WORTH MAKING

Acts 17:6b

"These men who have turned the world upside down have come here also." (ESV)

Freeway was a hit and the talk of the church. Pastor Eddie Bumpers preached it from the pulpit. "Get behind Freeway Ministries!" I remember one day during a sermon Pastor Eddie gave the people a challenge, and through that challenge he gained more respect from me than he will ever know. He said "We are supporting Freeway Ministries! This is a ministry of this church. If you have a problem with reaching these types of people then go find another church, because this one is not for you." I knew then that this was my pastor. He was 100% for what we were doing, and in my opinion, none of us had a clue what was about to happen with this ministry.

Freeway Ministries started because of three knuckleheads that were too stubborn to *not* believe that God could use them to turn the world upside down. The ministry was very demanding, rewarding, fulfilling, scary, and in a nut shell, one big adventure. We had business cards made and distributed them to places most ministries would never think of distributing them. We put them in the parole office, the jail, the homeless shelters, rehabs, and anywhere else we could reach those who needed it. We put our own phone numbers on those cards and passed them out everywhere we could.

I was the preacher and I was on parole at the same time. How many preachers do you know preaching on parole? I had almost two years to go before I finished out my sentence. I was working at the restaurant and slaving over a hot grill during the day, preparing sermons at night, answering the phone for Freeway, planning events, fundraising, working with men who were struggling, trying to be a single dad, and taking care of my little boy all at the same time. To be honest I have no clue how I survived all those things. Today I get tired just thinking about it all. Today's grace is not tomorrows grace friends.

I break a sweat thinking about all I would have to do in one week today, and I wonder if I could do it again if I had to. I am reminded of Paul's words in the book of Ephesians 3:7 "I became a minister according to the gift of the grace of

God given to me by the *effective working of His power*" (NKJV, emphasis mine). It was the energy which God supplied that kept me going. In my opinion, this is how the Apostle Paul kept going; it is the real reason people keep from burning out. I remember being afraid of failing many times. I did not think that I was good enough. God showed me that I wasn't, but He was.

In 2011 we started Freeway Ministries as a ministry of then Broadway Baptist Church, now Crossway Baptist Church. The ministry grew outside and above the expectation of anything that we had imagined. There is a verse that I turn to which reminds me of what God did through Freeway Ministries. Paul, the Apostle to the Gentiles said, "Eye has not seen, nor ear heard, nor entered into the heart of man the things that God has prepared for those who love Him" (1 Corinthians 2:9, ESV). That explains what God did to us in that little Baptist church on Broadway Street in 2011. He shook my world and turned it upside down.

I am going to share with you one of the most important events of my life: when I met my wife. I want to make something crystal clear before you go on reading this section: I would not recommend that anyone do things like I did. I almost lost my ministry and my family due to the mistakes I made. Let this encourage you, though, because God uses mistakes.

I had a mission to be used by God in this ministry and to work as hard as I could to honor God through my life. I had a serious weakness with women. I had no business being in a relationship as far as I was concerned, but God had something else in mind. Today, I share this with people who continue to shipwreck their lives through relationships. I am here to tell you that relationships are the number one cause for relapse. You can take that to the bank.

I was in a Sunday school class with the Mission's Pastor of the church, Paul Sheaffer, who would become a dear friend and a mentor to me. He was a great teacher and I was very eager to learn all I could from Pastor Paul. In that classroom, the second Sunday I was in the church, a man named Shad stood up and asked for prayer for his sister Sharla. She was a drug addict who had nothing left but an old rundown house and debt to his mother. Shad was telling the class that he was going to do an intervention on her. Shad talked with our leadership team and we gave him advice on what to do.

I remember we told him to take her phone, her car, and put her into a treatment center. I remember us telling him that she couldn't be trusted because she was an active drug addict. He listened to everything we told him. This conversation took place the week after the first Saturday night Freeway. Shad was excited to try to get his sister to Freeway Ministries the next Saturday night. We prayed and promised to pray for her, Shad, and their whole family. I had no clue that I was praying for the woman who would be my bride.

Shad, his brother Seth, and his mother Debby all made the trip to Ava, Missouri to do an intervention on Sharla that week. Little did they know that Sharla had just hit the floor in that little rundown house she lived in and asked the Lord to help her get off drugs. Ashlyn, her daughter, was living with her grandmother on her dad's side. Chase, Sharla's son, moved into his grandmother's home. They did the intervention on Sharla at her house and she was angry. She ended up going to detox, and then to her brother Shad's house.

Shad brought Sharla to Freeway, and she gave her life to Jesus under the preaching of the man who would one day be her husband. That guy was me. If you would have told me that this woman would one day be my wife I would have told you that you had lost your mind, but God had other plans. 1 Corinthians 2:9 says, "Eye has not seen, not ear heard, nor have entered into the heart of man the things that God has prepared for those who love Him." (ESV) God has a plan, and it is far greater than you and I can fathom.

I was paranoid about women and did not want to put myself in a position to be caught up in an unhealthy relationship, so I would place little kids beside me. I know that you are thinking "That sounds crazy," but you don't know the struggle that I had with unhealthy relationships. I had to set boundaries up, and sometimes those boundaries where Mike Aye's kids Coby and Macy. I would take the hymnal books off the church pew and place them on both sides of me, this prevented women from sitting by me. Do not get me wrong, I am not claiming that I have charming looks that women cannot resist. I am a rough, tattooed fella, who is overweight; I look kind of scary, but I was scared.

After Sharla gave her life to Jesus, she started coming to our church. I noticed her, and I thought she was beautiful, but I feared messing things up again. By this time, we had a Sunday school class for Freeway Ministries in the church. Sharla was there. She was staying with her biological dad and her stepmother on some days, then on other days she would stay with her brother Shad.

Shad took her phone, her car, and was making life hard on her. Little did she know, he was following our instructions to a tee. Not long after she had been coming to church, I noticed her staring at me. I always tell people she was stalking me like a tweaker in the bushes with a flashlight on their forehead. That wasn't the case though, she was dreaming about us being together, and her brother Shad had the same dream.

I am not a dreamer, and I am one hundred percent in agreement that God operates through His written Word. I also believe that God can do anything He wants. I refuse to put Him in a box. Our church was growing at a very high rate. We had three morning services. It was jam packed in that place. One day the ushers brought Sharla right to me and sat her by me. Of course, I had to move the hymnal books out of the way. Then Sunday night they did it again and again, the books had to be moved.

By this time, I was praying for a wife and a mother to my son, Keith. I would pick him up from preschool, and he would watch all the other kids get picked up by their mothers. He was wondering, "Where is my mom at, dad?" He would ask about why she wasn't around, and why she never came to see him. I was tired and worn out from ministering as a single dad. I remember talking to the Lord about Sharla. I said, "Lord if this is the one then places her with me again the next time we are at church."

That Wednesday night the ushers brought her to the middle row around five or six rows back from me. I thought, "Well I guess that means *no*, Lord?" Then the strangest thing happened. When trying to leave after the service was over, it was like trying to get over into traffic on the interstate at high noon in St. Louis, Missouri. There was a long line running along the church pews. I got out into the crowd of people as soon as I could. I got a glimpse of Sharla getting out way ahead of me. It might have even looked like I was running after her!

All the people that were between us somehow moved out of the way, and we were right next to each other. I wish you could have seen the look on my face when that happened. I thought "Okay bud you better make your move!" I got scared at first. Then all the sudden I had the courage to talk to this woman. It was a very strong back-and-fourth.

I did not even know Sharla's name yet. Before it was too late, I once again mustered up my sense of courage and chased her out the doors. This internal struggle of being sure I would ask Sharla for coffee when I got to her and then backing out seemed to occur a hundred times from the sanctuary to the parking lot. Finally, the moment arrived when I would have to decide which way I was going to go.

Running after her suddenly the most romantic thing I could think to say came out. "Hey, you want to go and have coffee sometime?" To my surprise she agreed. There was just one little problem. I had forgotten her name, so I had to call Rick Lechner to find out what it was. My sweet Sharla was a wreck of a woman, and honestly it is nothing but a stone-cold miracle that we are still married today. We had no idea how to be a couple and combining our past together created one big mess. The only reason that we have a successful marriage is because God is good, and we were too stubborn to give up. It didn't take long for me to start asking Rick the questions about Sharla that I should have asked before I jumped the gun at the church. Rick was the Freeway Ministries Sunday school teacher at the church and he is the co-founder of Freeway Ministries. I remember thinking to myself, "You don't even know this woman dummy." I didn't even know how many kids she had, or anything.

I started asking Rick over the phone, "Rick, does she smoke? Has she been divorced?" If you know me, you would understand the look on my face when I found out that she did smoke, and she had already been married and divorced three times. See I hate cigarettes and I promised myself that I would never marry someone who had been divorced. Here is the thing though, I knew I loved Sharla from the beginning and she was constantly on my mind and heart. I remember meeting Sharla's son Chase when he came to Freeway for the first time. I was always nervous about meeting people. I have insecurity due to all my tattoos. I thought, "I am going to make a good impression on this boy, and he is going to like me."

The day came and Sharla introduced him to me. "Chase this is John, and John this is Chase." I smiled and said, "Nice to meet you buddy." This 13-year-old responded in fear and tears. I thought, "Oh boy am I in trouble." Chase was outright afraid. His mom had dragged him and his sister through a lot in her addiction. In my opinion, Chase thought, "Here we go again!"

Ashlynn is Sharla's Daughter and she was graduating high-school. Sharla brought Ashlyn to meet me at Huhot, where I was a cook, during a lunch rush. Ashlyn had just had her wisdom teeth taken out, and she was not in the talking mood. I got the feeling that she wanted to cry as well. Here is the deal, both Sharla and I come from a very relationally immature background. Neither one of us had a clue how to have a healthy relationship. We made many mistakes and had to call Pastor Paul and have him help us with staying pure. I could preach a sermon. I could serve in ministry. I had no clue how to be a husband.

Marriage and courting was not something that I studied. My little boy was also in the middle of all this and had to share his daddy now. It had been Keith and I for almost two years. However, Keith loved Sharla and God gave him a mom. My son would no longer have to watch other kids spend time with their mom's and wonder where his was. That was one of the saddest things for me to have to see Keith go through. Not having a mom is hard stuff. Many women face the struggle of having their kids watch others interact with a father, and the whole time wishing that their kids had a dad of their own. I had to see Keith wishing for a mom; then, God gave us Sharla.

There were many times when I found myself in the W.I.C. office in a room full of women. I was the only dad waiting to get coupons for free cheese, milk, and bread. It was something looking at those mothers all alone with their kids. Then there was picking Keith up from the day-care and watching him look at all the moms loving their children, wondering where his mother was. I could almost see the expression on his face as a three-year-old little boy, "Daddy, where is my mom?" Now, he had one of his own, and this was an answer to my prayers. There was lots of work to do in my marriage to Sharla. Going from a drug addict to a preacher's wife in six months is enough to stress anyone out. I remember the day we came home from our honeymoon. My wife woke up after spending the first night in our house. I looked at her face and she looked afraid. She did not have a look of joy, excitement, or anything of that nature. I said, "You're scared, aren't you?" "Yes" she replied. After she said yes, she cried.

I asked why she was scared and Sharla replied, "I do not know." I knew then that we had a lot of work to do. To be honest I was a little scared as well. I had never been committed in a relationship. I always ran from every relationship that I had. I dealt with conflict by responding with violence and anger. I had a routine of getting up early, reading my Bible, and praying each day. I expect my wife to follow suit. My expectations were prideful and selfish, so much so that I forgot what I went through to gain the spiritual maturity I had. I was too relationally immature to give God time to work on my wife. I expected her to be machine, or something. I was about to face one of the most difficult tasks that I had ever faced.

Ashlyn, Chase, Sharla, John, and Keith

DISCIPLESHIP AND REFLECTION

I want to encourage you – guard your heart above everything. You need to be careful who you get into a relationship with. One of the things that I always say before I preach at Freeway Ministries is, "Do not come here to hook up in a romantic relationship but come here to hook up with Jesus." I see people fail time and time again due to the wrong relationships. You cannot undo some of the damage that has been done. Many times, people think that romantic relationships are the only kind of relationship. Trust me, this is far from true.

DISCUSSION QUESTIONS

Use these questions in a small group or discipleship setting. Answer your questions in a notebook following the reading of this chapter.

1. How many times have you failed due to a relationship?

2. How many people have you hurt because you tried to have a relationship when you were not ready, or the relationship was built on the wrong things?

3. How does the world see the idea of finding a wife, or husband compared to what God's Word says?

4. What do your boundaries look like in your walk with God? How do you personally plan to protect your walk with God?

5. Have you struggled with an addict in a romantic relationship? Think about the people that you were involved with. Remember, your boundaries are vital in any relationship with people, period. What are some specific boundaries you need to set prior to entering a romantic relationship?

REFERENCES

1. The title of this chapter comes from a book by Paul Tripp called "Relationships: A Mess Worth Making."

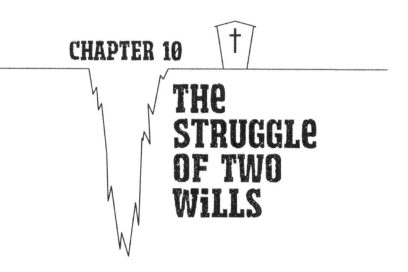

CHAPTER 10

THE STRUGGLE OF TWO WILLS

Ephesians 5:25
Husbands love your wives, as Christ loved the church and gave
Himself up for her. (ESV)

Romans 8:35
Who shall separate us from the love of Christ? Shall tribulation, or
distress, or persecution, or famine, or nakedness, or danger, or
sword? (ESV)

I intentionally used two verses that revolutionized my marriage. Through this chapter, I will explain some things that will be very transparent and even a bit embarrassing. The reason I am sharing this is because it is a part of my journey, and maybe someone can relate. You may know someone who is struggling, or you could be right in the middle of a war in your marriage right now. I hope that what I share will give you courage and hope for that marriage that seems impossible to redeem.

I remember coming home and the house was full of tension. My wife did not respect me, and I did not show her the love that she deserved. We were in a real spiritual war. It was a nightmare. We had a church face that we put on and when we arrived at the house we separated from each other. Communication was null and void! Everything she did made me angry and I remember thinking "My marriage is not going to make it." I continued to seek advice from Pastor Paul. I remember I would try, try, and try again. We continued to move forward and do ministry.

The ministry was growing, people were being saved, and God was doing great things outside of the home. Our home was another story. I wanted so bad to just have life, joy, peace, and harmony at home. We may not have been screaming, yelling, chasing each other around the house, but there was war none the less. I must admit that there was the occasional screaming. Honestly, I toyed with the idea of divorce, and I imagined what it would be like if we ended the marriage. Sharla did as well. We did not get it right until we were going on four years of marriage. We were like so many that come from the background of addiction.

Then one night, we had a breakthrough. I want you to think about something before we go any farther. How many major changes have happened in your life in an instant? You can probably count them on one hand. Statistically speaking our marriage should not have survived. My wife has been married and divorced several times, and none of them made it longer than four years. I am a man who has never been committed or responsible enough to be married. In my past I was too irresponsible to commit to anything. As soon as something came that involved hard work or responsibilities, I would walk away. I am not bragging about being irresponsible, nor am I proud of the fact that my wife has had divorce in her past. We were two lost people, addicted, and messed up. Now we were trying our best to have a successful Christian marriage.

On top of everything else, we are a blended family and my wife was a brand new Christian. I look back and see all the things that she went through in such a short period of time. She went from an addict, to moving away from her little country town, and then to living with her brother wondering what she was going to do with her life. Then she went from a serious drug addiction to a pastor's wife in six months! So, one night, after she and I had another night of misery, (I hope that you read that right. I didn't say *ministry* I said *misery*) I didn't know how much more I could take! Like Paul Tripp explains in his book, *A Dangerous Calling*, I was a preacher "Who was looking at himself through a distorted mirror."[1] I was not looking at myself through the mirror of God's Word, but through the mirror of the opinion and flattery of people, and success in ministry. My view was distorted, and I could not see that I desperately needed to repent and focus on the way I was treating my wife.

I was so in need for God's grace, but didn't see that need. I was treating my wife without the mercy and grace that I was so in need of. I was so focused on what she was doing wrong that I did not see my own sinfulness. I was not doing my job as a husband in God's eyes and my wife was hurting because of it. I was so tired of fighting, arguing, and the tension we called "normal." When I walked in the room, she was in her place in the bedroom sitting at the edge of the bed. You may ask "what do you mean by her place?" That is the place she would go to when she was hurt. She would go straight there and cry. Every time we got into a disagreement that is what would happen. It wasn't just her that had a place to run to. I had my place as well. My place was the head seat at the kitchen table. I would go there and study my Bible when I was hurting. I remember feeling so sinned against and disrespected. She was hurting so much, and she was just as frustrated as I was. We were lost, desperate, and didn't know what to do.

After seeing her I went to my place at the kitchen table and called my pastor to *tell on my wife*, as normal. Yep, that's right! I dropped the dime on my wife more than once! I often wonder what Pastor Paul thought of us each time I think back to those calls. I cannot help but smile, cry, and be thankful that God showed us grace through those difficult times. Paul told me, "You need to study what you're going through John." This was the beginning of the change in my marriage.

I bet he didn't even think what he said was a big deal, and honestly, I cannot remember much else of our long conversation that night. I am reminded of something that John Piper said, "Books don't change people paragraphs do."[2]

That night, a paragraph changed me in the middle of a long conversation. That one sentence changed my life. "John, study what you are going through." So, I got all my resources, all my notes, and my computer too. I began to seek out marriage, and God showed me something powerful that changed my life. I saw how the husband is the picture of Christ and the wife is the picture of the church. Right now, if your struggling in your marriage please stop reading this book and investigate Ephesians 5. Look at that picture Christ gives the husband to follow. Ephesians 5:21-33 describes Gods perfect design for marriage. That passage, along with the text in Romans 8:34-39, was instrumental for saving my marriage.

Just look at the example of a husband in the way Christ loves the church. As I looked at it that night, I thought "Who did the forgiving?" Then I thought about the sacrifice that Christ made. The way that Christ stuck it out with the church even though He was abandoned, and those He led did not believe in Him. I thought "God help me!" You may be thinking "I have read that verse before preacher."

Now, what I am going to share with you ate my lunch. In Romans 8:38-39 Paul teaches that nothing can separate us from the love of God which is in Christ Jesus. Inside the lines of those verses God convicted my heart. It says nothing can separate me from His love, and nothing can separate Him from me. Christ doesn't let things that come and go separate us from His love. He is the shepherd that holds the sheep. Those verses describe Christ's unconditional love that represents an unbreakable covenant. Paul gives a list of things that I was allowing to dictate the way I was loving my wife.

I realized that I needed to fight for my marriage. I thought, "Am I willing to carry the cross through thick and thin like Christ did?" Think of the covenant that Christ made without condition for you. Look back in the beginning, and picture God walking Eve down the aisle to Adam. According to the Apostle Paul the very first marriage in the Garden of Eden is a hidden treasure that pictures not marriage, but Christ and the church (See Ephesians 5:34-35). Think about the motivation that Christ had to go to the cross. His purpose was that the church would be sanctified and made without spot or wrinkle. Notice what the Scriptures teach in Ephesians 5:25-26: "Husbands, love your wives, as Christ loved the church and gave Himself up for her, that He might sanctify her, having cleansed her by the washing of water with the word." (ESV) Then I thought, "Do I care about my wife's sanctification? What kind of sacrifice am I making for my wife's sanctification?"

There I was sitting at the table broken over the way I was treating my wife. Then I found another verse that shook me to the core. This verse showed me that I was allowing things to separate me from loving my wife. Christ never allowed anything to separate me from His love! Read the verse Romans 8:38-39 "For I am sure that neither death nor life, nor angels nor rulers, nor things present nor things to come, nor powers, nor height nor depth, nor anything else in all creation, will be able to separate us from the love of God in Christ Jesus our Lord." (ESV) All the things that Paul mentions in the Scripture, that cannot separate Christ from loving us, were separating me from loving my wife! Have you thought about the way you love your wife? I knew right then that I needed to submit to Christ and love her like Christ loved the church. Then, and only then, would she follow me!

Right then I got up from that table and found my wife in the bedroom. I went into that bedroom and there she sat in the same place she always went when she was hurting, frustrated, and feeling unloved. I shut the door. I sat opposite of my beautiful wife. I read those verses to her sharing with her and confessed that I was allowing things to separate her from me loving her like a should. I then asked her a question. I said, "Sharla do you think that you could be a better wife?" She said yes with tears running down her face. Then I said, "Will you let me help you?" I asked her if she thought that I could be a better husband? If she thought that I could be a better father. I then said "Sharla will you help me?" This was the beginning of a new relationship that has turned us into a team.

We are now a team that serves the Lord together. Today my wife oversees the women's Discipleship Houses and is my biggest supporter and help, outside of the Holy Spirit. She has learned how to follow my leadership, and I have learned how to love her like I am called too according to the Scripture. We use these truths and experiences to grow together. So far, we have counseled so many couples that are at the end of their

ropes and that are ready to call it quits. Today, we experience revival in our marriage. We communicate to each other and are constantly learning more and more about each other every day. Those tense days are gone, and I am so glad about it.

If you're married or thinking of being married, please learn what a Biblical marriage looks like. I tell guys and gals that they should be able to sit down with their Bible and describe the rolls of a husband and wife. Before I

marry someone, I make them go through hours of premarital counseling with my wife and I. We go through everything that we have learned through our war for our marriage and all our struggles. That way they at least have the tools that they need to make it and a better chance starting out, than we did.

DISCIPLESHIP AND REFLECTION

Remember, the most important decision that you will ever make besides accepting Christ as your savior is the person you marry. Your spouse can limit you and your ability to minister, so please be very careful. Marriage is also a team effort. Both individuals must be sold out for Christ. And even with two people who are sold out for Christ, marriage can be extremely difficult. Satan wants marriages to fail. Satan wants your ministry to fail. Satan wants to create serious conflicts in the expansion of the Gospel, and he will use your marriage to destroy others. If Satan can destroy your marriage, then he can destroy your ministry.

DISCUSSION QUESTIONS

Use these questions in a small group or discipleship setting. Answer your questions in a notebook following the reading of this chapter.

1. In this chapter, I reflected on my own selfishness. What are some of the ways you have prevented yourself from looking in the mirror regarding your relationship with your spouse?

2. Go back to Ephesians 5:21-33. Read this text to yourself. What verses stick out to you regarding what Christ says about husbands and what Christ says about wives?

3. In Romans 8:35 Paul records a list of things that cannot separate us from the love of God that is in Christ Jesus. When you think about your marriage, or future marriage, how will you try to ensure that these same things cannot separate you from the love of your spouse?

4. Marriage is difficult. Christian marriage should symbolize a picture of Christ's love for the Church. In what ways are you going to commit to promoting this type of image? What can you do now to better symbolize this picture?

5. Christian marriage should look different than non-Christians marriage. When you think about this idea, how seriously do you take this calling?

References

1. Tripp, Paul David, "A Dangerous Calling." 2012, Crossway, Wheaton, IL.

2. "Brothers, We Are Not Professionals." Desiring God, 5 Apr. 2018, www.desiringgod.org/books/brothers-we-are-not-professionals.

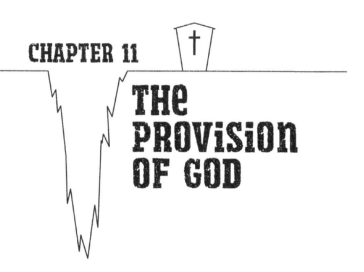

CHAPTER 11

THE PROVISION OF GOD

Philippians 4:11-12
Not that I am speaking of being in need, for I have learned in
whatever situation I am to be content. I know how to be brought
low, and I know how to abound. In any and every circumstance, I
have learned the secret of facing plenty and hunger, abundance
and need. (ESV)

In this chapter, I will share times in my ministry where God provided in ways that are hard to believe. If it didn't happen to me first hand I may even question what I am about to tell you myself. I cannot convince anyone of anything, but I can share the truth of my journey with you. God is my witness, along with my wife, friends, and family. These are some of the most precious moments in my life, and I hope that they are an encouragement to you as well. I have known how to struggle, and I have learned how to have things (Philippians 4:11-12). Those verses are close to my heart because they describe my walk with the Lord. I want to share the way God has provided for me since I started this journey in 2008 in that old, dirty prison cell in Fulton, Missouri. No matter where you are right now I pray that the Lord shows you His faithfulness through this chapter.

I lived in prison on $5 a month for eighteen months. Do you know what a person could buy back then for $5 a month? A stick of deodorant, five postage stamped envelopes, and one tube of toothpaste. Store day was once a week, and those of us who were indigent (poor) with no money got what is called a state tip. I call it prison welfare. I would have gotten $7.50 a month, but I didn't have a high school diploma, so they took $2.50 away from those of us who were not as educated. I guess they figure those who are uneducated should get less money.

We went to the store once a month and got what we could with our little bit of money. I remember to this day how it felt to watch others carry laundry bags full of food, soups, soda, crackers, and other things from the store into their cells when I had nothing. They would go to the store once a week, and I would go once a month. I was not jealous, and somehow, I had peace. Don't get me wrong, I would have loved to have family who sent me money, but that wasn't the case. Somehow God made me content in all things as the Scripture teaches us in Philippians 4:11-13.

There were folks in prison who would make pizzas out of ramen noodles, crackers, and summer sausage. Occasionally, my cellmate would look out for me, but I was still hungry! The thing that kept me full was the Word of God above my physical hunger. I had a spiritual hunger! There is a precious promise from Jesus in Matthew 5:6. Jesus said, "Blessed are those who hunger and thirst for righteousness, for they shall be satisfied." (ESV) Please do not miss what I am about to tell you. When you are satisfied with treasure in heaven you will not be distracted by the things on this earth.

Matt Chandler asked a question "Do your treasures have expiration dates?"[1] I was in prison, I was hungry, but my treasures were not on this earth anymore they were in heaven. I honestly believe that is part of why I was content. One of the things that I have learned is God answers prayer through people. He provided for me through a man named Rudy, the same Rudy from Chapter 7 that gave me the commentaries.

Rudy had been in the same cell for over twelve years. He was across the pod from me in the same cell block but upstairs. Our prison was a level four. That means the prison is one level shy of maximum security in the State of Missouri. We had our doors opened early and could move about through the cellblock if everyone behaved. Rudy and I struck up a friendship. He was also a believer. He noticed me, and I noticed him as well.

Rudy had a large collection of commentaries and aides that he used to study God's Word over his twelve years in prison. One day Rudy came to my cell and had a stack of papers in his hand. Those papers where printed commentaries. Somehow Rudy obtained those commentaries from the prison chaplains computer. He started sharing these commentaries with me. I had no idea what a commentary was from a hole in the ground. I devoured them! Remember, I was hungry!

It was like heaven on earth for me. It was a feast! Remember from earlier on all I wanted was someone who could help me understand the Bible and help to answer all the questions that I had. Looking back now with tears in my eyes I see that God used Rudy! Rudy was not the one to answer questions for me, but Rudy gave me those commentaries. I spent more time studying my Bible and reading those commentaries than anything else I did while I was awake. I learned so much from those studies, and I am forever grateful for Rudy and those commentaries. I talk with guys and gals all the time and tell them they can have as much as they want from God, but they must work hard in study. Unfortunately, people today are not willing to put forth the effort.

Since those commentaries came from the chaplain's computer they had no author statement, so I had no clue who the authors were. In one commentary the author was telling of a story that involved him. He mentioned his name, and I wrote it down. That author was Warren Wiersbe. I loved the way he explained things in a practical way. He helped me understand things, and I read all the commentaries that he wrote before I looked at any others. One day Rudy brought a stack of commentaries to my cell and as I threw them onto my locker he noticed I had no food. It was obvious to Rudy I was poor. You can tell in prison when someone is poor just like you can tell on the streets.

I will never forget the day that Rudy approached me. He said, "John, I want you to write me out a $10 list for this store day, so I can help you with your groceries." In prison you don't take nothing for free because that person will want something in return. I told Rudy that I would pass, but I was thankful for the offer. Rudy would not take no for an answer but insisted every day that I let him help me. Finally, he said "John, if you don't write me out a list of $10 worth of stuff that you need I am going to get you $10 worth of stuff that you don't need."

I remember that first store day as if it was yesterday. It is still vivid, and it's real to me. Rudy called me to his cell and gave me $20 worth of groceries, stamps, and hygiene products. He put it in a waste basket and I carried that waste basket to my cell with emotions at an all-time high. God was blessing me through His people (Psalms 5:12). Rudy kept that list and called me to his cell every single store day until I left that prison. I was in the prison for around 5-6 months, and Rudy became instrumental in helping me become who I am today.

I still talk to Rudy. When I was released from prison in 2009 shortly after I moved to Springfield, Missouri I started working. I got my first check for ringing a bell for the Salvation Army. I found a Christian book store and bought the complete New Testament collection from Warren Wiersbe. Then a short while later after I had enough money I bought the complete Old Testament. It was almost like I knew Warren Wiersbe myself.

I could read something he wrote and recognize his writing before I even knew he wrote the book. Today when I work with men through discipleship I always encourage then to get a complete New and Old Testament Warren Wiersbe commentary series. I share the story about that series growing me in a prison cell and, honestly, preparing me for the world of ministry.

In 2015, six years later, I was preaching a five-day youth camp for middle school and high-school kids. There was around a dozen plus churches there from all over the Midwest. I quoted Warren Wiersbe in my sermon, and after the sermon a pastor approached me. His name is Gary and he pastors a church in Lincoln, Nebraska. I will never forget the conversation that we had. He said, "I noticed you quoted Warren Wiersbe in your sermon." Then I proceeded to explain the story of Rudy giving me those commentaries, and how I spent my first paycheck on his complete New Testament. I explained how I got his commentaries for young preachers that come through the ministry. Then Pastor Gary said something that floored me. Gary said, "How would you like to tell him that story yourself?" I said, "Are you kidding me?"

He explained that he was a friend of Warren Wiersbe and they met together in a men's group often. They lived in the same city and he said, "If you're ever in the area let me know and I will try to get a meeting set up with you two." Right now, as your reading this book you may say "That is a neat story, but I am still a little skeptical on the fact that God made this happen. This could be a coincidence." I left a small part of this story out. This camp meeting was in July, and one month later we were launching our fifth Freeway Ministries location in Omaha, Nebraska. I had planned a trip to Omaha in August to support Rick Lechner who is a cofounder of Freeway Ministries. He was kicking off the Omaha Freeway, and Omaha is right around the corner from Lincoln.

One month later I was sitting in the living room of the man who wrote those commentaries. God's grand design planned all this for me. I was looking in the eyes of the saint that has sold hundreds of thousands of books that help people all over the world. I shared with him that he helped me understand the difficult things of Scripture (2 Peter 3:16). I shared my story with Mr. and Mrs. Wiersbe. In six years I collected many of his works, and he signed them all! Can you believe it? I was in the house of Warren Wiersbe! He took me into his basement and walked me through his private library. He was in his 80's and still writing books! Betty and Warren Wiersbe prayed for me! I will never forget that day and I will cherish the moment forever!

Warren Wiersbe was such a blessing. I still cannot believe I could go into his private library and see his collection of books. In his library where he still writes he has a bed, bathroom, desk, and everything else he needs to live in that library. God provide a real miracle that day to have Mr. and Mrs. Wiersbe pray for me in their own home. I email Mr. Wiersbe from time to time, and he continues to pray for me. Who could have ever planned this? This was something that only God could have planned.

I met Pastor Gary at this camp. He introduced me to Warren Wiersbe.

John and Warren Wiersbe

John in Warren Wiersbe's Private Library

Relaxing in Warren's Living Room.

REFLECTIONS AND DISCIPLESHIP

God does not haphazardly throw things together. He has a plan according to His purpose for things to work in a way that will glorify him (Ephesians 1:11). God also brings people in your life to teach you and to mentor you, and He does so for a purpose (2 Timothy 2:1-2). God used Rudy and Warren Wiersbe to mentor me both from a distance and from close personal contact. He has provided people in your life to build you up and to strengthen you so that you can be His witness to the ends of the earth.

DiSCUSSiON QUESTiONS

Use these questions in a small group or discipleship setting. Answer your questions in a notebook following the reading of this chapter.

1. In this chapter we explored the truth that God brings people in your life for a reason. As you look back on your faith journey, who are individuals that God has used to guide you in truth?

2. I never expected to be able to meet an individual who had done so much to strengthen my faith. Have you had an encounter with someone who has built you up from afar? How amazing has it been to acknowledge God's divine hand in working these things out?

3. Warren Wiersbe was present in the place that he was not. How much of a motivator is that for you to have an impact beyond your physical location?

4. Looking back at the importance of using the resources God has provided you, what can you do better to take advantage of the resources God has granted you to grow in the faith?

References

1. Chandler, M., & Wilson, J. C. (2013). To Live Is Christ, To Die Is Gain (p. 136). Colorado Springs, CO: David C Cook.

CHAPTER 12

GOD SUPPLIES ALL OUR NEEDS

Psalm 50:10–11
For every beast of the forest is mine,
the cattle on a thousand hills.
I know all the birds of the hills,
and all that moves in the field is mine. (ESV)

Philippians 4:19
And my God will supply every need of
yours according to His riches in glory in Christ Jesus. (ESV)

Before I was married, I remember moving into a barn with my little four-year-old boy. That barn was remodeled for me and it was amazing! It didn't have hay or farm animals, and it was very livable. Marsha and Terry Courteous were very kind to allow me to live there and trusted me to live next door as a neighbor. God not only provided a place to live but a huge help with childcare. Shortly after moving into the barn I was married, and we became a blended family of five. We all lived in the barn. Freeway was being used by the Lord in mighty ways beyond our vision for it. God was using a bunch of misfits for His glory and honor!

Freeway took off and we were all riding by the seat of our pants. My weekends were gone, and every night my time would be spent on the phone trying to build relationships with the community and of course trying to save the world! This went on for almost two years. I was working at the restaurant as much as I could to earn an income, teaching in the juvenile on Tuesday nights, preaching on Friday, Saturday, every other Sunday night, newly married, raising a blended family, discipling men, adjusting with a wife who was six months sober, and learning how to be a leader of a non-profit ministry. Talk about pressure!

My friends from the Bible study, Rick Lechner and Mike Aye, were right there in the middle of the fight with me along with other families that stepped up. We would not have made it without them. I look back at that part of my life and realize that it is God's grace that enabled me to make it through those times. During the time of developing Freeway, my only source of income was my job working in the restaurant. I made very little money there and could only work 25-30 hours a week due to the ministry responsibilities. It was hard on everyone in my house.

I would see my family very little and Sharla helped me so much with Keith, who was four when we were married. I remember many times we did not know what we were going to eat that week. I was too prideful to tell anyone at the time, but God saw us through. Sharla got a job working for Marsha at the daycare and we were scraping by. One day a man called me from our church. I could tell that he was broken by the tone in his voice. He asked me a question "John, I need to ask you something personal" he said. "How much money do you make a month?" I thought, "That is a strange thing to ask a man." He continued to explain "My family saves money to support a ministry every year, and we have decided to use it to put you into fulltime ministry."

He invited me to come and have coffee with him and talk about it. I went and met with him, and he explained the burden to help me. He said, "God has burdened me to do this John. We want to free you up to do what God has called you to do in ministry." He had the first check in his hand as we spoke. I turned it down and pretended to be fine. I was not fine! I was hurting, and God burdened this man to help me. This was the Lord busting open a door to answer prayer, and I was too proud to allow Him to help me. I will never forget the walk from the coffee shop to my car.

The whole ride to the barn I thought "That was the dumbest thing you have done all week!" Before I move on let me make something very clear to you. Pride in leadership is your number one enemy. You must be willing to accept help when God sends it. Remember to accept gifts from people who have the gift of giving. Eddie Bumpers (my pastor) told me something one day. He said "John, people who have the gift to give usually have the gift of discernment." Something you will read throughout this book is that God uses people to answer prayer. Most prayers that have been answered in my life have been answered through God's people.

I walked through the doors of the house and said to my wife, "Sharla, do you trust me?" Can you guess what her reply was? She said "John, you're going to quit your job, aren't you?" She was scared and started to cry. Looking back at what she went through in such a short period of time I am full of respect for her because she did not run away as fast as her legs could carry her. I explained the whole situation to her and we were both nervous about the decision. The thing that was nerve racking was the fact that my friend could only pay my salary for four months and after that I would be on my own. Freeway Ministries had four months to cut through the red tape and get it together.

I went to work that next day and it was miserable. I knew that I should have said yes to my friend. I knew that I was not supposed to be there anymore, and my pride had caused me to say *no* when it should have been *yes*. I worked out my shift and went home. I made the call and rescheduled another meeting with this gentleman. I shared with him the pride in me saying no, and I let him know that he was really an answer to prayer. I shared everything with the board of directors, and they said I could accepted the help from him. He said "put in your two weeks and let me know when you're finished working them out. After that we will have a check for you."

I couldn't believe it! I was really going into fulltime ministry. The next day I turned in my two weeks. A thousand things could go wrong, but we were trusting in God. I will never forget what I am about to share with you. This was one of those times when God Almighty moved in a way that only He could. It was a couple weeks or so before Christmas and our first Christmas together as a family. My wife and I had been married since April of that year. We had about thirty-five dollars to our names, and that included the change on the dresser if you know what I am talking about.

I called my friend to get my first check and he was out of state. When he told me "I am in Washington, so give me a couple weeks to get back to you and I will have it." My heart dropped to the floor, and my wife was just staring at me. The look on my wife's face was the *you are supposed to be the leader* look as I broke the news to her. She just cried and said, "All I want is to be able to have Christmas for my kids John!"

Remember there was only thirty-five dollars in our bank account. I wanted to cry with her, but I knew that I had to be strong. I remember telling my wife "We must pray and trust the Lord, Sharla!" That is what we did and God showed up. I am reminded of the verse I shared at the beginning of this chapter. In Psalm 50:10-11 God speaks the truth that He owns everything, and He is not needy for anything. I know today that this God, who is rich in resources, will provide my needs. This was one moment, among many, that I have asked the Lord not to let me forget.

I was at church a few days later and Rick Lechner came up to me with an envelope. I had no clue what was in it, but Rick said some old man had given it to him for me. Another saint of God who I will not mention gave my wife a card as well. When we were driving home we pulled over and opened that envelope. It was $1,500 cash and the card had a check for $500 cash in it. I don't know where that envelope came from, but I know who sent it. It was my Father who laid the burden on someone's heart to answer our prayers and meet our needs.

We just cried and thanked the Lord. Our kids were watching us from the backseat of the car. I pulled the car over and shared a testimony with them. My wife and I told them that this was the Lord looking over our family. We made sure that they knew God was taking care of us and answering our prayers. I told them "You boys better never forget this! We were hurting and trusted the Lord and He has done this!"

There have been times when I walked outside to my car to leave and there were one hundred-dollar bills laying in my driveway, literally scattered around in front of the door of the barn. I remember running into the house "Sharla look at this! This money was just lying in the gravel in front of the door!" How can you explain five hundred dollars just lying in front of the door in the driveway? During times of struggle people would call me and ask me to go and have lunch with them. I would go, and they would tell me "The Lord has burdened my family to help support your family. Here is some money." God used those moments to humble me. I learned that God will supply all our needs, but not all our wants. He takes care of us when we walk by faith.

Many times, when speaking of contentment, I have come under heavy conviction for myself and for the Western Church. We are very spoiled and take many things for granted. Paul writes under the inspiration of the Holy Spirit about contentment. 1 Timothy 6:8 "If we have food and clothing, with these we shall be content." (NKJV) Notice, that Paul doesn't mention a house to live in. Let that sink in. Does that trouble your heart? Food and clothing is all that Paul describes in necessity for the believer.

The way I see it is I have always been poor. I was poor and didn't even know it most my life! Something happened that I nor my wife saw coming. We have had private support from some individuals for most of our ministry. There were people who have been led to help us financially only because the Lord laid a burden on their hearts. As I have said before, I struggled with accepting help, but I have learned that God answers prayers through people. One person has helped us many times with love gifts, out of the blue and just in time, without even knowing it.

Now before I go on and share this part of my journey please note that I never asked for this. I didn't put personal financial needs on social media, sent a prayer request, share a burden, setup a go-fund me account or anything. I was content living in the barn and had no idea what was about to happen one Sunday after church. Our friend who has been a regular blessing to our family called me Sunday on my way home from church. This friend said "Hey, can I come over to visit after church? I have something to share with you." I thought "Praise the Lord! I get to feed a saint of God!"

I asked, "What kind of food do you like?" I ran to the store and bought a nice cut of steak, and all the fixings. I started cooking and was preparing the meal when our friend showed up. After small talk and sitting down at the table our friend looked at me like a parent looks at their child and said, "I am going to share something with you and you are not allowed to interrupt or say anything." That is hard for me, because I am a preacher. I sat quietly thinking "What in the world is going on here?" As I type these words I must pause because of the overwhelming memory of God and His goodness to me! As my son would say "These are happy tears."

This person with a mouth full of steak whips out their Bible and notebook. Then the person began to share Scripture after Scripture with me. The Scripture was all about being there for one another and how we should bare each other's burdens. I remember looking at my wife and thinking, "what in the world is going on here?" Then our friend said "John you and Sharla have been living in this barn long enough! Everyone else has a home of their own except you! I believe that you need a house of your own."

Then this person threw a stack of papers on the table in front me. I can almost hear the thud it made as it landed on the table to this day. I said, "What is this?" as I flipped the stack of papers over. Our friend said, "They are homes listed throughout Springfield." I turned to my wife, and she was a crying mess. I said, "We cannot afford a house payment." I was only making $1,200 a month and had three kids at home. My wife worked part-time at a preschool. My friend said, "I have prayed about this for a whole year, and I know that this is what God wants me to do."

The words came in a parental tone again, and I knew that my friend meant business. I just sat and listened as they spoke, "I will buy the home, and you can pay me back. You pay me whatever you pay to live in this barn. If you ever move or get called away from here, then we will work something else out."

Then there was a knock at the door. I looked at my wife like, "What in the world is going on?" People usually didn't just show up at our house unannounced. It was a realtor! The realtor said, "Are you ready to go and look for your new home?" Here come the tears again! It is still hard to share this without breaking down. We drove around for a couple weeks until we found the home that we felt like God wanted us to have.

We moved into our home and loved it. It was just over a year old and on the end of a cul-de-sac. Understand that no one in my family that I know of has ever owned a house. We rented all my life, and here I am with a home of my own.

Someone who never had credit buying a house without even applying for a loan! The house even had a privacy fence around it! I remember going to Walmart stoked at the fact that I was about to buy a water hose. I remember asking the guy at the lawn and garden "I need the best hose and the best holder for it as well."

I wonder today what I looked like to him holding two different water hoses in my hands excited to purchase a water hose saying, "Which one is the best?" in my excited voice. He most likely thought I was nuts. Either way, it was a big deal to me and is still a big deal today. Sharla and I are forever grateful for the people God has placed in our lives! God has provided in so many ways, and if you remain faithful He will provide for you what you need, but not always what you want.

REFLECTIONS AND DISCIPLESHIP

It is not easy to step out in faith. Freeway Ministries is an outpouring of numerous people stepping out in faith to do what God has called them to do. True evidence of a changed life is not only that one leaves the old ways behind, but they step out in faith to do what God has called them to do. God's Word is clear. He is in control. Sometimes however, it is difficult for us to see the blessings when He provides them. We struggle with personal pride and sometimes dismiss those He has given us to be the hand of Him provision. When we refuse to accept God's provision we demonstrate that we are truly trusting ourselves rather than God who owns "the cattle on thousand hills" (Psalm 50:10). We must all trust God to provide.

DISCUSSION QUESTIONS

Use these questions in a small group or discipleship setting. Answer your questions in a notebook following the reading of this chapter.

1. Where in your life do you need to confess pride so that you can receive the blessings God has already provided?

2. What does it mean for you to acknowledge that God will give you what you need rather than what you want?

3. Identify a time in your life when you have seen God provide for you in an amazing way? What was it and how did it change your situation?

4. Maybe you are one who could be a blessing to others, how can you *better* an individual who God uses as His hand of provision in the life of another person?

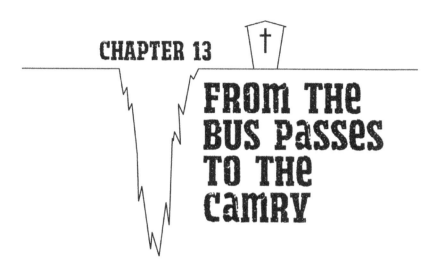

CHAPTER 13

FROM THE BUS PASSES TO THE CAMRY

Luke 12:29-31

And do not seek what you are to eat and what you are to drink, nor be worried. For all the nations of the world seek after these things, and your Father knows that you need them. Instead, seek His kingdom, and these things will be added to you. (ESV)

God has provided for me from the first day of learning the bus routes, to Dewey Huston, to my job at HuHot, my wife, and Keith. God Almighty was with me. Many times, the only thing I had was a Biblical view of the Lord and faith in His promises, and that is all I needed.

The Scripture in Luke 12:29-31 pertains to this section of my journey because I wasn't seeking anything but the

Lord. I was not worried about monetary things in my life or material things (Luke 12:22-34). I was seeking the Lord for all things.

I landed my job at the Huhot Mongolian Grill, and the bus was my only means of transportation. Every day except Sunday, I would wake up before the sun came up and walk in the dark to that bus after studying the Bible. The Harbor House was at the bottom of a big hill and in a rough part of the city, but I never had one problem walking to the terminal at 6:00 a.m. I didn't even see it as a struggle at the time.

As I look back I realize that it was grace from the Lord that gave me the strength to continue through that time in my life. After I moved out of the shelter I continued to ride the bus for a couple more months from my little house on the corner of Nichols and Fort. All the way on the northside of Springfield to the southside of Springfield to the Battlefield Mall, where Huhot is still located. I had money saved from working at Huhot and I was constantly putting all that I could in the bank.

I remember thinking, "If I didn't have to rescue my son from this situation I would still be living at the Salvation Army riding the bus and saving my money." Mona and Leron Wagner, owners of the Huhot, along with Dewey, helped me get to my out of town appointments and court dates. I was working hard trying to accomplish all the things that the State of Missouri wanted me to finish to gain custody of my son. I attained the Cadillac from Dwayne and got it legal. Let me say that I got a 100% on my driving test as well. Who says miracles don't happen anymore?

The Cadillac was a great car for me, but one day I was going to change a flat for my soon to be wife, and I was t-boned at the gas station. I had a Freeway van to drive for a while and went through several used cars. As I said earlier, God uses people to show us favor and answer our prayers. Eventually, Freeway Ministries agreed that I needed a business vehicle for all the driving that I do while working for Freeway. We had a donor offer to give me a car to drive. This car was nice, but it kept breaking down on me and often I would have to take my wife's car. We would get the car fixed, but not too far down the road it would break down again.

The ministry doesn't have a lot of money, but we do have faith in God to provide. The final straw happened on a Friday afternoon. I had a prisoner to pick up from Algoa Correctional Center in my home town of Jefferson City. Jefferson City is a little over two hours from Springfield. I had to preach at our Friday night Freeway once I got home. I have a friend who is a retired truck driver named Allen Greenfield who asked if I needed company. Allen and I left bright and early in the morning. I was excited to pick up this gentleman from prison. I am always fired up to be the person to pick up someone from prison.

My favorite part is taking them for their first free meal. I didn't have the pleasure of someone doing this for me, but it is awesome to be that guy to do it for someone else. We picked Tim up bright and early and headed back to

Springfield. We took Tim to get a big fat greasy sandwich and headed home. I was a little over an hour from Springfield and stopped to use the bathroom. Allen said in his country accent, "Boy I smell something coming from the car! Are you sure this thing isn't over-heating?" I looked at it and it was a bit hot. I thought, "I will get this thing rolling down the highway and the wind will cool it off."

I now think, "Why did they let me make that decision about the car?" I am not a mechanic by any stretch of the imagination. I can cook, clean, preach, counsel, but as far as fixing cars, I am not your man. We headed down the highway and the light came on, so we pulled over on the side of the road. I said, "What are we going to do now?" I had a few hours to make it to preach at the Friday Freeway and we were on the opposite side of Lebanon, Missouri. That makes it two hours to drop off Allen in Marshfield and get to the church to preach. Allen, Tim, and myself got out of the car. We lifted the hood and tried to figure out what was happening with the vehicle.

This is where my good friends begin to laugh knowing my abilities under the hood. Allen said, "It is overheating and losing water. If we can get some water in it maybe we can make it to my house and you can use my car." I thought "Where are we going to get water at?" Tim just got out of prison hours ago and there is no telling what he thought. Then I had a bright idea of taking off the cap to let it cool off faster. Allen went to release some of that pressure and the cap shot off, hitting the hood, and falling under the engine. It was trapped in the undercarriage in a place that none of us could possibly reach.

As we looked around and thought about our situation Allen said "Hey, there is water in that ditch! If we can find something to put that water in, we can fill up the radiator with water and take it slowly down the road!" That is what we did. We drove a volcano for two hours down the highway. We would pull over at gas stations and let it set. Then we would drive until it got hot and then pull over again. We would put water in it over and over. I finally got Allen dropped off and left my car at his house.

I arrived at First Baptist Church Springfield just in time to preach the message that night. It was a close call and the last one I would ever make in that car. God has provided us with mechanics that volunteer their time to work on our cars, vans, and buses at Freeway. We have several friends who are gifted in that area. One of them picked up that car and towed it to his shop. Meanwhile I was driving a loner. Then a friend approached me. He said, "If you could have an SUV or a car which one would you want?" I know this person has a true blessing from the Lord and I had a feeling where he was going with this. I said, "I am good with the car we have. It is in the shop, and I think it has some more life left in it." I was being prideful again, and honestly did not believe the words I was saying.

I have no clue why I act that way when God is trying to bless me. This is a struggle I have had my whole walk with God. I struggle with accepting gifts. The Lord is persistent and so was my friend. After a minute or so I said, "A car would work just fine." The reason I said that is because I knew a car was less expensive. They said, "We want you to be able to go and preach without having to worry about your car breaking down on you. Go to the dealership and tell them you want a brand new Toyota Camry."

You must realize that just eight years prior, I was released from prison with nothing but a card that had $5 on it. I have never had anyone in my family own a brand-new car. We looked up the pricing for this car and I talked the salesman down around $4,000 under the asking price. I will never forget that day and I will never forget the way that God has provided for me and my family. I asked that they donate the car to Freeway instead of giving it to me and they did just that.

Driving away that night I remembered all the vehicles I drove throughout my lifetime and the cars my mother had growing up. We had a car called "The Dragon Wagon" as a young man. I remember being so embarrassed of that car that I would make my mom drop me off a block away from school and the skating rink. We would make up rap songs about my mother's car; I remember being so humiliated by that big green beast. There was the van I drove that had no air conditioning and a hatch that would not open. There was the purple van that read "Ozark Assembly of God" on the side of it. Here I was, a man who had been homeless most his life, strung on out drugs, in and out of jail, redeemed and saved by the loving grace of God, driving off the lot with a 2016

Toyota Camry completely paid for. I could have never purchased that car on my own or would I have even thought it possible.

Through God's provision I have a reliable car that can take me to preach revival meetings, to plant Freeway Ministries outreaches, and to travel all over without the concerns of the car breaking down. I am reminded of Ephesians 3:20, "Now to him who is able to do far more abundantly than all that we ask or think, according to the power at work within us." (ESV)

REFLECTIONS AND DISCIPLESHIP

Sometimes there are hurdles the road. They can be a broken down car or a messed up plan. God shows Himself to be good, even during times of trials. As you move forward in your pursuit of Christ there will be times where you will be inconvenienced to do what is right. God shows Himself in these trials and through these trials to be sufficient. You never know where the next blessing is coming from or what it will be.

DISCUSSION QUESTIONS

Use these questions in a small group or discipleship setting. Answer your questions in a notebook following the reading of this chapter.

1. What are you doing now to prepare for the trials that are ahead of you?

2. What blessings have you already seen show up in unexpected ways as you have pursued Christ?

3. As you look back on your journey in your pursuit of Christ, what are some steps to little moments that have taken place where God has shown is amazing provision?

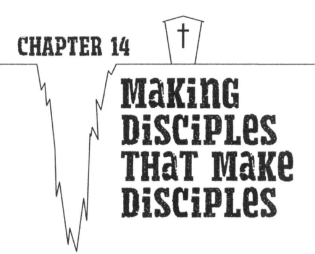

CHAPTER 14

MAKING DISCIPLES THAT MAKE DISCIPLES

Matthew 28:18-20

And Jesus came and said to them, "All authority in heaven and on earth has been given to me. Go therefore and make disciples of all nations, baptizing them in the name of the Father and of the Son and of the Holy Spirit, teaching them to observe all that I have commanded you. And behold, I am with you always, to the end of the age." (ESV)

2 Timothy 2:1-2

You then, my child, be strengthened by the grace that is in Christ Jesus, and what you have heard from me in the presence of many witnesses entrust to faithful men, who will be able to teach others also. (ESV)

"Christianity without discipleship is always Christianity without Christ."— Dietrich Bonhoeffer

Making disciples was not an option to Jesus, the Apostles, or the early church. Why is it so foreign today? Freeway Ministries takes pride in making disciples of Christ. Not a *look at us pride*, but a *look at what God is doing through obedience to His Word* pride. We boast in the Lord for what He is doing through our ministry!

I was not discipled by any man and it almost cost me and disqualified me from ministry before I started. I had no clue what I was doing as a single man in Christ. I had my little house on the Northside of Springfield. I was going to church when the doors were opened. I was plugged in to the local church, a men's ministry, and serving everywhere I could, but I was not discipled. Dewey Huston was a solid mentor to me, but I needed someone to get into my business!

I am forever grateful for Dewey, but discipleship is more than what we had. Discipleship is every day practical principles, and disciplines used in everyday life. Discipleship is learning the doctrines of the Bible, and then being instructed on how to apply them to your life. Discipleship is practical application to a man or a woman's life. Matt Chandler says that "Discipleship is not just transferring information but transferring a lifestyle."[1] My brother-in-law. Shad McGuire, had some discipleship material that they used at his old church. It was not anything new, but it was effective, so we used it. We began to work with individuals that would make a profession of faith. They were new believers who gave their hearts to Jesus at our outreach meetings.

We began to bridge the gap between the two people groups,[2] those in church and those outside the walls of the church. I see it as a meshing of the two people groups together. We had a meeting at church with as many mature Christians as we could get. We held the meeting and tried to get them fired up for discipleship. We had no clue what we were doing. The idea was that a mature Christian would meet with a new Christian on a non-church night for an hour and a half. They would begin to go through the Bible using the discipleship material as a platform to build a solid foundation.

We were in for a rude awakening. We found that many would come to the altar, claim to be saved, shed big tears, but were not serious about following the Lord. Our first year in discipleship we wore out our disciple makers. Many who made decisions were like bad employees who did not want to work! Some of them were harder to track down than America's Most Wanted. That year was rough! We saw many finish their discipleship and that was awesome, but many of our teachers were burned out and done. This is when I learned the valuable lesson of what is commonly called *obedience-based discipleship.*

When Jesus said "follow Me" what happened if they didn't? How many people in the Bible did Jesus drag or push? Jesus called men and women to follow Him, but they had to do the work. This is obedience-based discipleship. Think about what would happen if Jesus told one of His disciples to get in a boat because it was time to move on and they didn't get in the boat. How would that situation turn out? I can tell you how it would turn out, friends. Jesus would leave them on the bank of the lake and He would be on the boat headed to the other side without them.

We were making it too easy on them. There was a way to weed out those who were not serious! So we began to use this method for discipleship! When someone would tell me that they wanted to be discipled I would tell them, "Show me." I would have the person come to the meetings through the week and prove that they wanted to be discipled. One of the things that I say to this day is, "If you put the same amount of effort into following Christ as you did feeding your addiction, nothing will stop you." Some would say "I don't have a ride." Some would say "I was tired after work." Then I would say "Did you have excuses why you couldn't pick your dope up when you were in addiction?"

It is also important to know that we provide transportation to most meetings. Those who are serious will not make excuses, but show up. You must make them do the work or they are not read; you'd be spinning your wheels. This is for the parent who is struggling or the loved one who does not know what to do. Take it from an old junky who has been transformed by the power of Christ. MAKE THE PERSON DO THE WORK!

After we started making people put some effort into their discipleship things changed! For instance, if someone wants a ride to go look for work, instead of giving them a ride we give them a couple of bus passes. We are still helping them, but it makes them do the work. It takes effort to get around on a bus, but they are showing you they're serious by getting out there and doing it. Many people were finishing their discipleship and the accomplishments were not without notice. The parole officers, judges, and even police officers in Springfield noticed a change in people they knew from streets.

We started making certificates and presenting them to our people at our meetings. It was awesome to see and still is to this day! We have seen hundreds discipled through our ministry, and many of them are now discipling others. What began as seven names on a list and some men praying in a coffee shop, developed into something only God expected! Discipleship has been one of the main things that has changed our partnering churches, and one of the things that make Freeway Ministries different than most others. We have averaged of around 75 successful disciples every year since 2012.

What if your pastor asked the church, "If you have been discipled raise your hands?" Do you think that very many hands would be raised? I would honestly say most people in churches would not be able to say *yes* to that question. My people group are those who have a background of addiction and crime. Those folks, for the most part have very little knowledge of who God is. They need help breaking free from the Hollywood idea of God! The cultural view of God is distorted and twisted. We work with our people and teach them the disciplines and principles of God's Word. We also teach them how to apply it to their lives. All the way from the basics of God's Word to the judgement seat of Christ.

By the time they are done with discipleship they understand why they give, how to deal with sin, how to deal with others in Christ, worship, prayer, the person of the Holy Spirit, the world system, Baptism, the Lords Supper, and so on. They are committed to learning for a minimum of fourteen weeks. After they are finished they become someone else's teacher and they start to make disciples.

Three points of discipleship is something that I learned since God has allowed me to be in ministry. Let me share them with you! The first step is finding yourself a Paul. In 2 Timothy 2:1-13 Paul is writing to his son in the faith, and through this letter we get to see into the heart of a disciple maker. Paul tells Timothy to find faithful men who can also teach others. See Paul was saying "Timothy, find yourself a Timothy." Timothy found a Paul and now Timothy was to find someone who was just like he was when he met Paul. The second point is find a Timothy after you find a Paul.

Before I move on to the last point in discipleship I want you to ask yourself a couple questions. Have you found a Paul? Have you found a Timothy? I am going to write later about the people I have met on my journey, and the many unique stories that have come from the ministry I have been blessed to be a part of. One of the things that I often come across is men and women who come to know the Lord, but never find a Paul. Many develop the lone gun Christian mentality and never reach their full potential. Many fall away and never get plugged into the local church because they refuse to make themselves vulnerable. Many fall away, get bitter, or upset because the church will not conform to their idea of what ministry is supposed to look like.

I was fresh out of the Missouri Department of Corrections and just getting used to going to church. I was making some friends, but all the friends I was making were just like me. The church that I went to had an outreach that ministered to those in addiction, and I was more than interested in that ministry. I was there when the doors where open. I met lots of people and many of them would not go to church on Sunday or Wednesday when the "normal" people where there. There lies a great divide and many will not cross the line. I was one of those who went to church every time the doors were open. I was afraid though and embarrassed of the man I used to be. One of the things about me is that I cannot hide my past due to the tattoos all over my neck, hand, and face.

I remember one day when I shared with those who were a part of the recovery group. I said, "I know God has called me to be a preacher." Then one of the other brave souls that would shadow the doors of the church on Sunday morning said, "How are you going to be a preacher if you will not talk to anyone?" I really could not answer that question.

Please don't miss what I am about to share with you. If you're reading this and you are like I used to be in church or know someone who can relate, I have a word for you. Make yourself vulnerable! You will never find a Paul without making yourself vulnerable. I looked for the godliest men in that church and I opened myself up for rejection. I shared it all with them and I was rejected by some but was accepted by many. Doug Thomas was one of the men that helped me grow in the Lord! He preached and taught Sunday School class. There was a bigger difference between me and Doug though, because Doug was a cop.

Doug was a cop, through and through. He was also one of the godliest men I have ever met. He was a cop and I was a convicted crack dealer, but he cared about me. That is what mattered the most. Remember the more mature Christians you can get close to and learn from the better off you are going to be. You also want to find a Timothy as well. There are many people in the church that have not found a Timothy. They are like the Dead Sea and have nothing going out of them. They are just keeping everything that they have experienced to themselves.

You know what lives in the Dead Sea? Nothing! Many church members have spent years just keeping all the knowledge, experiences, and lessons learned to themselves. Young Christians are sitting right there in the church that are about to make huge mistakes in their lives and they walk past them every day. The Bible does not suggest discipleship; it *commands* it. Be like the hardworking farmer, and work hard at planting the seed into those who are hungry to learn the Gospel. Look for those who are faithful and invest in them.

Make sure you find the right motivation. I remember many people who signed up to be someone's discipleship teacher. They are all kinds of excited about it and cannot wait to take part in the Great Commission. Then the person they are working with falls away or relapses. They get discouraged and get another person assigned to them. The next person does well, and then they fall away. The disciple maker gets discouraged and they quit. They may not say, "I quit," but that is what happens. I want you to ask yourself a question. Ask yourself, "What keeps me going?" In the ministry that I am in, I see so much heartache, disappointment, and hurt, but also blessings. I have learned the same truth that Dewey Huston must have learned years before I met him. The motivation that must drive us in ministry is the faithfulness of God. That, my friends, is the key! When I ask folks what their motivation is, they usually say fruit, obedience, joy, or something to that extent. Those things are good, but those things will not endure like the faithfulness of God.

Think of the prophet Jerimiah for a second. Remember his ministry? Where was his fruit? Where was his joy? That scripture I shared from 2 Timothy 2:13 is vital to this truth I am sharing with you. Look at what Paul wrote in the context of discipleship and enduring as a soldier or hardworking farmer "if we are faithless, He remains faithful— for He cannot deny Himself." (ESV) God cannot deny Himself and is faithful to His Word.

Discipleship is the heartbeat of God and you cannot go wrong being in the middle of obedience to God's heartbeat! I know if my heart is right, and I am being obedient to the Lord, then He cannot do anything but bless me. God blesses us when we are doing the things that His Word calls us to do! It does not make me happy when someone fails, falls away or goes back out into the streets. I think of every person that walks away, and my prayer is for them to come back to the Lord, but them falling away doesn't stop me from reaching out to the next person.

If your motivation is people succeeding, then when people stop succeeding you will stop being obedient to the Lord. God does not always let us see the fruit from our obedience. You have no idea how God is going to use those seeds you planted in a person's heart. That is none of your business. God doesn't owe us an explanation and He doesn't owe us details either. Many times, when we see the fruit of someone coming to know the Lord it is the increase from someone else's hard work and labor. Paul, the disciple maker of all disciple makers, said it best 1 Corinthians 3:6-8 "I planted, Apollos watered, but God gave the growth. So neither he who plants nor he who waters is anything, but only God who gives the growth. He who plants and he who waters are one, and each will receive his wages according to his labor." (ESV)

REFLECTIONS AND DISCIPLESHIP

One of the greatest accomplishments in ministry is seeing someone imitate you as you imitate Christ. Seeing someone you poured into pouring into another person and then seeing that person pour into another is a beautiful thing. That is what discipleship should look like. You cannot force another person to be a disciple maker nor can you force someone to be disciple. Discipleship is an act of submission and obedience to the Lord. It is a commitment between you and the Lord first and foremost. If you are serious about following Christ, then you must be serious about discipleship.

Discussion Questions

Use these questions in a small group or discipleship setting. Answer your questions in a notebook following the reading of this chapter.

1. The author noted in this chapter, "The motivation that must drive us in ministry is the faithfulness of God." How does this apply to being discipled and discipling others?

2. When Jesus said "follow me" He did not drag the disciples along after that. Think about those who are discipling you. How did they make their offer to disciple you?

3. As you grow your faith, you will find Timothy's of your own to disciple. Based upon the example of Christ and based on the example of those who are discipling you how do you plan to approach the ones the Lord will one day call you to disciple?

4. The Bible teaches very plainly that we are to be disciples that make other disciples. How do you plan to work within your church to help promote discipleship?

5. As you reflect on those who are discipling you, what attributes of their life do you admire the most? What spiritual disciplines do you feel are their strengths? How do you plan to imitate your "Paul" as you become a disciple maker?

References

1. Chandler, M., & Wilson, J. C. (2013). To Live Is Christ, To Die Is Gain (p. 164). Colorado Springs, CO: David C Cook.
2. I call folks who come from drug addiction a people group. Those in addiction, crime, or an unchurched background.

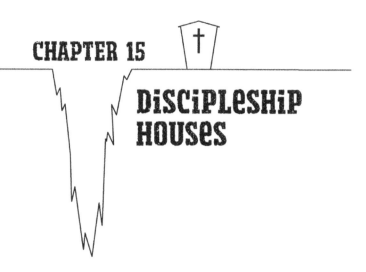

CHAPTER 15

DISCIPLESHIP HOUSES

1 Timothy 1:12-16

*I thank Him who has given me strength, Christ Jesus our Lord,
because He judged me faithful, appointing me to His service,
though formerly I was a blasphemer, persecutor, and insolent
opponent. But I received mercy because I had acted ignorantly in
unbelief, and the grace of our Lord overflowed for me with the faith
and love that are in Christ Jesus. The saying is trustworthy and
deserving of full acceptance, that Christ Jesus came into the world
to save sinners, of whom I am the foremost. But I received mercy
for this reason, that in me, as the foremost, Jesus Christ might
display His perfect patience as an example to those who were to
believe in Him for eternal life. (ESV)*

As I sit here at my kitchen table remembering, those times in the homeless-shelter, I recall the fears, the concerns, the worry, and the desire to succeed in life for the first time. I remember the old holiness preacher, Jim Snell, and his unique way of leading. Before there was a Freeway Ministries there was a structure that I learned to follow. The structure was developed while living there at the shelter and God used it to keep me from falling. Let me make something clear for a moment. I cannot give credit to a structure for keeping me from falling, but the God the structure was devoted to gets all the credit. Jim Snell is a big part of who I am today, and I am very thankful for the investment that he made in my life.

After planting Freeway Ministries, Mike, Rick, and I decided that it was time to open a recovery house. Rick had a desire to do this and so did I. Mike Aye had a desire to help people and was on fire for whatever the Lord had for him to do. The church where Freeway was birthed had been in a building program when we first started. Now the church was moving to their new location just a few miles away. There was a little house on the far end of the property that the church owned. The pastor agreed to let us use it for the first recovery house. Freeway had outgrown that same house during our first meeting. They used it for Freeway Sunday School. It was just empty, so we began to remodel it and turn it into our very first recovery home. We called it "The Discipleship House."

We had guys who knew construction well and they were a true blessing to the ministry. Too many helped to name them all, but they were hard workers who put their backs into it with a passion for the Lord. We got our first house ready to go and filed our paperwork with the City in 2013. What was going to happen? We didn't have a clue, but the Lord did.

We had this idea of bridging into the local church and pouring into the local church with the structure like I had been a part of in the shelter. We also housed some classes in the evening taught by men from the church. The idea was to place eight to nine men into a house and give them a structure to live by that is hard to follow, and strict enough to weed out those who are playing games. I have learned that you must make it hard for them to fake it.

A place like this would have been a dream for me when I came out of prison. Everything I learned from the moment I was released from prison I applied to this structure. With the help of the other brothers that co-founded the ministry, we started something that would change many lives. We took concepts from the living environment in Cuba, Missouri where I lived for twenty-one days to the Salvation Army Harbor House. Everything that was effective for me in the shelter, my past as a criminal, and the wisdom from the men God placed in my life was used to develop the discipleship housing.

For me, it was a dream come true. Finally, I had a chance to better help people who were like I once was. Rick Lechner had many things in common with me and for years he had wanted to do something like this. His dream was more of a recovery center; later this came true for him. We learned so much from that first Discipleship House. The things that I learned you cannot learn in a classroom.

There is no class in college or in seminary to prepare you for the things that come from opening something like this. I have dealt with about every kind of scenario that you could possibly imagine plus more. I learned that you cannot always tell who a good leader will be because leaders rise up out of the group. Sometimes those who you think will be the best leaders end up flaking out on you. People hurt you, fail you, and are faulty because they are people. That is why we must always place our faith in a perfect God, because people are people.

We group eight to nine men in the same house, all of them on probation or parole. We teach them how to live like adults and how to hold each other accountable. Most of these men have been raised by people who had no clue on how to be a parent. These people come to us very immature and in need of a lot of help. One man is the house leader and he has no fees to live in the house. He has his own bedroom but has a greater responsibility. He is the one who is my eyes and ears. He also is the one who everyone goes to when they have a problem. This man is the spiritual leader of the house.

Let me give you a brief version of the structure that these men are to follow. Let me put it to you this way, if most of the members inside the local church had to follow the structure we ask our people to follow many would not be able to make it through the program. Every day, these men are to get up early in the morning and spend time in God's Word.

They are to place five job applications in every day until they get a job. They are to be at church when the doors are open. If they miss church they get kicked out. They are expected to give back to the ministry an hour for every hour they are ministered to. They must give half of their week to ministry.

Our folks are in a class every night of the week besides Tuesday night. We have two classes that are taught during the week in the evening by men from the local church. These classes are open to the public and have everything to do with learning more about the Gospel and growing as a man. We do book studies and then when those book studies are finished we recognize our people with a certificate publicly. Our men are not allowed to be in a romantic relationship of any kind while they are in the program. Let me say that includes emotional relationships as well. Talking, texting, Facebooking, being alone with or even sitting with a woman at church is not allowed.

You may be thinking right now "Man, that seems really harsh preacher." This is literally a matter of life or death. I tell them all the time "You are not here to meet your wife, find a good job, and make a lot of money. You are here for the duration of the program to prepare you for the rest of your life. That is the purpose of the program, and you must focus 100% on your discipleship." Relationships are the number one cause for relapse. They are to focus 100% on the things of God for the season of their lives that they are in the Discipleship House. We are training up men of God who will shake the world with the Gospel. Our people are learning how to handle conflict and how to settle disagreements without killing each other.

These men began to go into the local partnering churches and embrace the preaching of the Gospel. They start serving in the local church and soon enough they start ushering. Some of my church friends who are reading this now are saying "Ushering in the church?" I said ushering in the church. These men and women who have been lifelong criminals are now learning that they have a purpose, and they can be more than someone who shows up and goes home in the local church. These folks are now *serving* in the church.

Can you imagine a guy who is a convicted drug dealer that has never been in a church being asked to usher? This was something that happened because of a man named Mike Melton. One day Mike started having these men help with the ushering. Mike has been a part of Crossway Baptist Church before it was Crossway. He is a church guy with a tender heart that has been in the church since 1979. Can you picture that in your mind? Ex-cons and recovering addicts handing the offering? Well that is exactly what was happening.

People loved them and then it took off like a wild fire. We planted another house and another house. One after another the houses fell in place. We have our graduates all over the place serving the Lord and being an example to all those who know them. Our people are on the mission field, in the Bible colleges, private investigators, and even preforming surgeries in well-renown hospitals. We have had pastors, refugees, and even professional golfers in the houses. They are in the choir singing, on the stages preforming, in the pulpits teaching and preaching the good news! It has been amazing to see God using our people to change the world.

As I write this my burden is to open a house or two every year. Today we have an average of around 48 disciples in our houses in two states. That is not including the house we have opened in South Africa through Lakeview Community Church. We are saving the tax payer $1.8 million dollars a year just in keeping them out of prison for the duration of the program. That does not include working, paying taxes, keeping a job, staying off drugs, and leaving the life of crime.

Today we have three houses in Springfield, a ranch in Marshfield, a center in Omaha Nebraska, and as of June 2017 we launched Freeway Ministries, Cape Town, South Africa. You are probably thinking "How in the world did you get to Africa?" That is for a later chapter, but we did none the less, or should I say the Lord did it! Let me share how God supplied the need with no interest and no money down.

John and some of the ladies from our
Discipleship Houses.

Discipleship Houses Thanksgiving
2017.

Discipleship house, Omaha,
Nebraska, ran by Rick Lechner.

Our first international Discipleship
House, Cape Town, South Africa.

Freeway Ministry disciples in Cape Town, South Africa.

REFLECTIONS AND DISCIPLESHIP

As I had stated at the beginning of this chapter, structure was exceptionally important when it came to getting my life right. It wasn't the structure however that made things right for me it was God who used that structure to get me thinking correctly. The demands in our Discipleship Houses is exceptionally difficult, but without the structure one is left to their own devices. I cannot emphasize enough just how important it is to be disciplined in your study of God's word and being around right people. That is what the Discipleship Houses are supposed to get you thinking about. With that said, serving the church by giving back to the war is of invaluable significance.

DISCUSSION QUESTIONS

Use these questions in a small group or discipleship setting. Answer your questions in a notebook following the reading of this chapter.

1. What does it mean for you to have structure and discipline?

2. How valuable is it for you to be part of the local church?

3. How can you do better at giving back to the local church in various forms of ministry?

4. When the chapter talks about various places that graduates of the Discipleship Houses are now serving, what amazes you most?

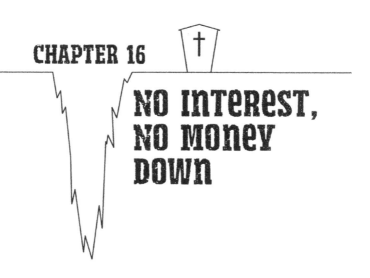

CHAPTER 16

NO INTEREST, NO MONEY DOWN

2 Samuel 12:8

And I gave you your master's house and your master's wives into your arms and gave you the house of Israel and of Judah. And if this were too little, I would add to you as much more. (ESV)

Romans 8:32

He who did not spare His own Son but gave Him up for us all, how will He not also with Him graciously give us all things? (ESV)

These Scriptures describe the truth that I am going to share with you. What I am going to tell you is as just as much a miracle as any that you may have heard. Freeway Ministries had been going strong for two years and we were breaking into 2015. We knew that there was a desperate need for a women's Discipleship House. We had around $60,000 in the bank at the time. I had no clue on how to buy property, get a loan, keep a mortgage, or anything of the sort. We had no credit that you could write home about and I was less than three years off of parole. The insurance company even refused to insure the board of directors unless Rick Lechner and I were removed from it due to our criminal background.

We had grown from one Freeway outreach to two Freeway outreaches in the city. We had our Friday Freeway location in the worst part of Springfield, Missouri at the time. Many that come from my background were raised by a single mother. I was a mama's boy my whole life, and most of my friends were as well. I have always had a heart for single women, and have seen the effects of drugs on their families.

Here is how it works many times. The woman ends up pregnant with the baby and the father goes to prison. She loses the kid due to her addiction and gets pregnant again. She loses that kid and gets pregnant again. That is one example. Here is another common example. The mother gets with the guy, and he goes to prison off and on for the next ten to fifteen years. He gets out long enough to get her pregnant again, and goes back to prison. Either way, children are forced into this situation.

These kids grow up in the environment that their parents create for them. Where do you think those kids end up? What do you do about it? Well we decided that we were going to target a certain group of women. The group of women that we were targeting were the ones who had been separated from their kids and had a chance to reunite with them. We prayed and prayed about this. We had a friend who was a realtor and we began the hunt for the next Discipleship House for women who had been separated from their children. We had that little bit of money in the bank. The search was on and we began to look for the house.

We were praying, looking, dreaming, and hoping for the best. It was a bit nerve racking and in a short bit of time I learned a lot about looking for a house. Little did we know that God had one already picked out for us. Our worship leaders, Grant and Anna, were being called into full-time ministry. Grant was talented with anything that had to do with technology. He designed our website and he was a talented musician. Anna was a beautician and a fantastic vocalist that came through the ministry due to a brother who gave his life to the Lord through Freeway Ministries. Adam was the drummer of the band and they made an amazing team.

Anna and Grant were very young, but they were also very mature. They were more mature than most Christians I know in their 30's and 40's. They are like my kids, and I have had a strong bond with them since before Freeway started. In 2009, during my first year of preaching, Adam came to know the Lord and was changed from an angry young man to a kind young man. The change was so dramatic that Anna and

Grant having no drug history became part of the crowd from early on.

Grant and Ann placed their house on the market around the same time we started the process of looking for a house for our ladies. They sold their home fast. They had a big surprise for Freeway Ministries. Anna and Grant gave Freeway Ministries 100% of the profit from their house to put toward the women's house. Can you believe that? They are in their 20's and gave close to $30,000 to Freeway Ministries. Then, out of the blue, a missionary from Nicaragua, who I became friends with, called me asking if we wanted to buy his house. He was asking a very low price for his home. The only problem was that it would take all our money that was in the bank to purchase this house.

Notice that the chapter is called "No Interest, No Money Down." I had developed a relationship with a couple through applying for a grant from a bank. I had a friend tell me about the possibility of this bank giving us this grant. I called her, and she explained that this grant was given once a year by a local bank, but they were not a Christian organization, though she herself was a Christian. She informed me that I may have a better chance getting the grant from the bank if my letter of request was less about Jesus and more about our needs. She was a kind and godly woman who was just being honest about the situation but to me it was a test from God.

I thought to myself, "Man, we could sure use this grant!" I also thought, "What is most important?" I wrote the letter and made sure to include Jesus multiple times. I thought I would rather be rejected by men for putting too much about Jesus in the letter then deny my Savior. We did not get the grant. You may be saying to yourself, "Why would you put that part of the story in this book then?" The reason is through this lady came a strong relationship that would affect me and my family for the rest of our lives. Turns out they had a family member who struggled with addiction his whole life and they were seeking help. This couple ended up coming to Freeway Ministries and their family member also started coming as well. We built a strong relationship through that phone call about that grant and one day they called me into their office.

They asked me if I needed some money to purchase the women's house. I told them yes, and they said, "How much?" I told them, and they wrote the check then and there. The check was for over $50,000! I was driving down the road with a check for over $50,000 and we never had to borrow a penny.

We own our women's house and our men's house now. Two houses with the sole purpose of helping men and women start their lives over. We had a whole new battle to fight with women who have been dragged through the cycle of addiction, crime, abuse, and abandonment. I found out why there are more men's houses than women's houses, fast and in a hurry. Women are way harder to deal with then men. I am not just saying that, it is a fact.

If you're a woman and reading this, you are secretly saying "You know that's right!" If you are a man and reading this, you probably don't get it unless you have been in this type of ministry. The women we targeted came with emotions that the men we were dealing with didn't have. None of the men we had, carried a baby in their bodies and then had the child taken away. This effects a woman in ways that men cannot understand and is very unnatural. God's design and purpose is shattered because of the sin of addiction, and with that comes lots of baggage to work through. There are many more complications with women than there are men in recovery. Guess who dealt with the women when they had issues, conflicts, or someone had to be asked to leave? Our wives did. My friend Jim Corbet told me, "Sharla doesn't have your personality and things are harder for her when it comes to dealing with discipline. Remember John, your wife is not like you." Our policy is women minister to women and men minister to men. I would go and deal with the men's Discipleship House on a regular basis. Conflicts, hidden sin, disagreements, asking people to leave, confrontations, working through different struggles, etc. With the women, my wife would have to go with Rick's wife Sherry.

If you could see my face right now you would ask "Why are you smiling?" My wife was not and is not a confrontational person. She is an introvert, or at least she was before she married me! When I think of my wife I think of a baby bunny rabbit. The first time that there was an issue at the women's house I had Sherry come pick up my wife, and I will never forget that moment. I was on the phone with Rick and said, "Have Sherry come and get Sharla. They can go and confront the ladies together." Then I looked over at my wife and she had the look you get when someone pours freezing cold water down your back on a hot summer day.

Sharla looked at me and said, "Why are you doing this to me?" I said, "Honey, do you want me to find another woman to do it?" I knew those words had a good chance to make her brave and not give up. The structure in the women's housing is similar to the men's housing. Sherry and Rick have now moved up north to start Freeway in Omaha Nebraska. Sharla and Jessica Merrick have done an amazing job of overseeing the women's housing.

Along with many other women who volunteer now through the ministry, we have success in our women's discipleship housing. Sharla has grown in ways I never imagined for her, and she has had so many people help her along the way. Today, Sharla is bold and brave like never before. She is doing things that she never thought possible, and it is all because of God's mercy and grace. God has surrounded us with people like the mountains surround Jerusalem (See Psalms 125:2). Jessica Merrick has been a real asset to Sharla helping with all of the tough stuff that comes with handling this type of ministry.

There are so many ladies that come and teach on Monday's and Tuesday's that make up the hands and feet of Jesus as well. We have seen real life change through our women's house and family after family restored! These ladies are overcoming odds that you do not hear about in churches. Women who have been sold as sex slaves, who have never had a job, drove a car, had horrible upbringings, and never shadowed the doors of a church are changing in our community through the program. God knew what He was doing when He burdened us to start our housing ministries.

REFLECTIONS AND DISCIPLESHIP

It is easy for women to be overlooked in recovery ministry. While reclaiming one's family often begins with men, there is an equally important aspect when it comes to ministering to women in recovery. God's word is clear that men and women are different (Genesis 1: 27). Evidence for this distinction has been clearly observed through the work of Freeway Ministries. Recognizing that men and women are different is vital to a Christian understanding of the world. This concept is also important when it comes to effectively reclaiming one's life and family for Christ.

Discussion Questions

Use these questions in a small group or discipleship setting. Answer your questions in a notebook following the reading of this chapter.

1. Psalm 100:3 states, "Know that the Lord, He is God! It is He who made us, and not we ourselves . . ." God has designed men and women differently. How might this distinction between male and female be a critical element to understanding your very own recovery?

2. Throughout this book it is very evident that God supplies one's needs. In this chapter, the author was faced with a decision to proclaim Christ at the expense of losing possible funding. How might one prepare themselves effectively for experiences similar to this?

3. At Freeway Ministries, one of the key elements to dealing with the recovery of men and women is that men minister to men and women minister to women. Why do you think this decision is so important?

4. In this chapter a young family was mentioned because of their maturity and their sacrificial giving. What are some key elements of spiritual maturity and how does one connect spiritual maturity with sacrificial giving?

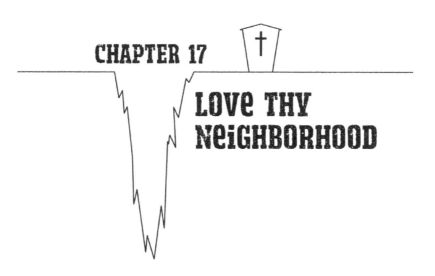

CHAPTER 17

LOVE THY NEIGHBORHOOD

Matthew 22:34-40

But when the Pharisees heard that He had silenced the Sadducees,
they gathered together. And one of them, a lawyer, asked Him a
question to test Him. "Teacher, which is the great commandment
in the Law?" And He said to him, "You shall love the Lord your
God with all your heart and with all your soul and with all your
mind. This is the great and first commandment. And a second is
like it: You shall love your neighbor as yourself. On these two
commandments depend all the Law and the Prophets." (ESV)

      This Scripture is one of my favorites and it applies to
many areas of my personal ministry! I have had to remember
this for many reasons through tough times, valleys, and the

loneliness of leadership. Just imagine Jesus, who walked the earth as God in the flesh, being confronted by religious people. These people not only confront God in the flesh but are testing Him with questions about the greatest commandment. Jesus gives them two commandments that are not even part of the *big ten*. Jesus explained that the everything hung on these two principles. First, loving God with everything you have. Second, loving your neighbor as yourself. That word *hang* used in the Scripture gives the picture of a door hinge. Just like a door without a door hinge is not effective, so those who know the law without love for God and their neighbors are not either.

I want to share a time in our housing ministry where I felt like the world was crashing down on me. It was time for us to open another men's house. We had two successful houses, and a major need to open another one. We had calls coming from every prison in the State of Missouri, parole, and probation as well. To be honest, if we had ten houses, we could fill them up, the need is so great. We even had rehabs asking about housing, but we had no more room in our Northside men's house.

God was using this discipleship structure for His glory and honor. We began to pray and seek God's wisdom. The City of Springfield placed a moratorium on sober living houses. Then the attorney for the City of Springfield who led this moratorium left the City so we were stuck. Many of you are saying "what in the world is a moratorium?" They were not allowing anyone to open anymore recovery houses in the

City until the City figured out what planning and zoning would allow. This placed the recovery community in an uproar because it violated the Supreme Court ruling that passed in 1988 when the Oxford House won against the State of California.

The City of Springfield refused to allow anyone to open recovery houses. They were refusing all applications so we decided to go outside city limits to the County to avoid the conflict. I called our realtor friend and informed them that we were looking for another house. We have a good friend who is a lawyer and we were ready to pull the trigger and fight. He knew beyond a shadow of a doubt what the City was doing was against the law and we would win.

Searching and searching for property in our anticipated spending range was exhausting. I learned more about real estate than I ever thought I would learn in a short time. We found a giant house on the Southside of town in a decent neighborhood. It was perfect and we offered around 15,000 under the asking price. My relator friend said, "Are you sure that you want to go that low?" I replied, "Yes, that is all we can afford." Of course, they turned us down and countered. I turned the offer down and told her to tell them that was the only offer we had. She looked at me like, "This is not how you do real estate." Little did she know I had no money to buy that house, but I knew God led me to make the offer. I also knew that God would help us raise the money.

Later after we had stopped searching they called us about the house and took the offer. The relator was just shaking her head. There was one problem though. We didn't have $145,000. Now you are probably thinking, "That is irresponsible of you to do something like that!" My response is show me the verse that backs up that way of thinking. We had prayed and had some options, but we were not sure of what we were going to do yet.

I called a friend of the ministry that offered to help us. They agreed to loan us the money, and I went to meet with them. Not long ago I was living in a shelter, but there I sat in the office of someone who was going to trust me with a check for $145,000 on a hand shake! Can you believe that? They wrote the check and said, "We do not need to draw up the contract just yet because we trust you. Take the check and go get the house."

That day I walked out of that office with a check for $145,000. I was on my way to the title company with almost one hundred and fifty thousand dollars in my hand! I was shouting, crying, praising, and so overwhelmed that I had to pull the car over. I will never forget the day as I walked into that title company and saw my buddy Mike Aye. He was sitting there with a big smile on his face and I felt like I was in a dream. Just an old junky from Jeff-City holding a check for $145,000 not including the fees as well. I had a check in my hand to buy a second house for our men! Praise the Lord from whom all blessings flow!

This reminds me of the Scripture in Ephesians 3:20, "Now to him who is able to do immeasurably more than all we ask or imagine, according to his power that is at work within us," (NIV). I have no clue who is reading this, but I promise you that God's Word is sure and true! How can anyone explain something like this? There is more to this story, though. Our friends who had loaned us the money drew up the contract for $160,000. They had agreed to allow us to get the house started before we began our payments. It was getting close to our first payment and our friends called me into their office. They canceled the debt and gave us the house. They canceled the debt to the house! We owned three houses and God was allowing us to do more than we could ask or think.

REFLECTIONS AND DISCIPLESHIP

In Romans 12:18 it says "If possible, so far as it depends on you, live peaceably with all." (ESV) Working to live peaceably with others sometimes results in one being inconvenienced, but this is one of the most effective means for one to demonstrate that they love their neighbor. As a believer one is called to submit to governing authorities because they are instituted by the Lord (Romans 13:1-2). Loving one's neighbor and submitting to the government go hand in hand. One of the most important elements of loving one's neighbor and neighborhood is demonstrated by the way one submits to God's word as the ultimate authority. God blesses those who honor Him and His teachings, and when you live in submission to God's Word it changes your neighborhood from the inside out.

DISCUSSION QUESTIONS

Use these questions in a small group or discipleship setting. Answer your questions in a notebook following the reading of this chapter.

1. One of the distinctive marks of a Christian is that they submit most importantly to God's word. At times, living in submission to God's word creates inconveniences for us in our society. How might you prepare yourself to live in total submission to God's word despite dealing with inconveniences?

2. In this chapter the author noted that he desired to "live peaceably with all" (Romans 12:18). Because of this desire, he chose not to engage in a legal battle with local government entities. When is it a good time to walk away from a conflict even when one knows they are in the right?

3. What does it mean to love one's neighborhood?

4. How can your local Christian community be more effective in demonstrating their love for their neighborhood?

5. How can you individually demonstrate that you have a love for those who live in your neighborhood?

References

1. See Fair Housing Act of 1988, Oxford House versus the State of California.

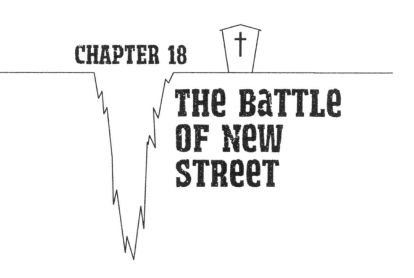

CHAPTER 18

THE BATTLE OF NEW STREET

Psalms 3:6
I will not be afraid of many thousands of people who have set themselves against me all around. (ESV)

Things were moving ahead with Freeway Ministries and God was blessing our work! People were being saved and lives were being changed in a radical way! Our houses were going great as well. We had numerous testimonies of victories through our women and our men. We desperately needed another men's house. By this time the applications were coming in from just about every prison in Missouri, but not only prisons. There were many rehabs, hospitals, homeless shelters, and concerned family members sending applications in as well.

There was a tragedy in Springfield were a little girl was abducted from the park on the west side in front of witnesses. The story was and still is horrific to our community. This man did horrible things to this little girl and then killed her. This sent fear throughout our city. The city went after a certain organization that had similar housing as us. They are way different in their structure and they accept registered sex-offenders. They were under serious attack and the newspapers were adding coals to the fire. They put what is called a moratorium on any group-home residence in the city. The problem with that was I knew that the City was breaking the law.

I had studied this for years and had my friend Jim Corbett, who just happened to be one of the top lawyers in Springfield, on my side. He also was read up and prepared for the fight. We purchased our last property in the County because we wanted to be friendly with the City of Springfield and not cause any problems but they were leaving us no choice. The city attorney who put the moratorium in place moved and now the city didn't know what to do. They had meeting after meeting over this but nothing changed.

In a federal lawsuit in 1988 the state of California lost against a group that paved the way for ministries like ours. There is a statue called the Fair Housing Act of 1988, Oxford House vs. the State of California. The Supreme Court made a judgement that eight to ten addicts could live in a single-family residence if it had the proper size because they agreed that the benefits of the structure and accountability gave addicts a better chance of succeeding in recovery. The City of Springfield made a ruling that no more than three unrelated people could live in a house together in a single-family zoned residence.

There was and is today a desperate need for structured housing for men and women in every city across our country. I have buried multiple people from overdoses and had to follow my God given conviction to open another house. We leased the property a couple miles from the City Square and it wasn't long before the gloves came off. The city came against us and tried to shut us down.

I will never forget the phone call from one of our house leaders. Josh called and said, "You won't believe what happened today! The city posted a sign in our yard!" I heard the words and cannot help but feel my neck tighten up just reflecting on the conversation. I said, "What did it say, Josh?" Josh replied, "It reads, 'You have thirty days to move out of the house or the City of Springfield is going to shut your power off on all three of your houses, and take all of your permits from you.'" I thought "Oh man! God has given me a great responsibility of shepherding these men and women! What will we do if they shut us down? What will happen to our people? They are going to be homeless because of me." Josh said, "There is more! They also are threatening the owner of the property that we are leasing from. They say that they will shut off all the power to his properties as well!"

I personally knew that the people we leased the New Street property from had hundreds of properties throughout the Springfield area. I thought "There is no way that they will stand by us on this!" I called our lawyer and told him what was going on and he said, "So it begins!" I was very concerned! He said, "John, they cannot do this and if they do we will take them to court.. I will write them a nice letter letting them know that I represent Freeway Ministries and if they so much as touch your lights we will see them in Federal Court."

I called the property owner that I thought would fold on us and he said, "I am standing with you on this." I could not believe it! Not taking anything from the owner but he had a lot to lose. However, he stuck by us on this deal. We were fighting the third largest city in Missouri! Turns out that one of our board members is connected to the utility company. He called them, and they said, "The city cannot do that to you!" Our lawyer sent a nice message to the city and they backed down!

That house was open for a year. It served its purpose for us and we have seen three men in that year make it successfully through the program from that house. At the end of the lease we decided to opt out of the contract, and take another opportunity to open a bigger house in the country. These men are pillars to the community and disciples of Christ today! This was the first time that we had clashed with the City and I am sure that it will not be the last. There are many who use recovery houses to make money and have little to no structure. I understand where the City is coming from. Some people are in it for money and some are in it to help people change their lives. Just like anything there are good and bad people in every line of work.

With that being said, what are we to do with folks that have addiction issues that get released from prison? Are we to segregate them from society? Tell them that they have to live with "family" that are blood related like the city stated? What if their blood related family are all criminals and drug addicts? We need to understand that there are ways that do not cost the tax payer money, and alternatives that make a difference in our communities. Remember, when you are doing something for the Lord not everyone will agree with you and you will face opposition.

Society, at large, believes once a criminal, always a criminal, and once an addict, always an addict. We believe that the Bible teaches freedom in Christ and that God stands behind His people when we walk by faith. Be encouraged brothers and sisters that God fights for you.

John, David Gidcumb, Greg Craig

John and David Gidcumb sharing at a school in Cape Town, South Arica

REFLECTIONS AND DISCIPLESHIP

There are certainly times when one has to give a defense. Scripture clearly calls us to, "Honor Christ the Lord as holy, always being prepared to make a defense to anyone who asks you for a reason for the hope that is in you; yet do it with gentleness and respect" (1 Peter 3:15, ESV). Part of recovery is recognizing, with discernment, how best to defend your Christian faith, and how to share that faith. Adversity in your Christian walk often presents an opportunity for you to demonstrate the change in your life and to share the Gospel. This assault on the Freeway Ministries presented an opportunity for Christians to demonstrate how they conduct themselves in a society that is often hostile towards them.

DISCUSSION QUESTIONS

Use these questions in a small group or discipleship setting. Answer your questions in a notebook following the reading of this chapter.

1. How can you know when it is appropriate to act in defense of your Christian faith and ministry?

2. What are some examples from Scripture where an individual was called to act in defense of their faith?

3. When God is moving in the lives of others there is often a pushback from Satan. Read Ephesians 6:12. When you read this verse, how does it impact your life?

4. Read Ephesians 6:13-18. When you consider the assaults that will occur in the near future as you continue in your spiritual walk, which weapons of spiritual warfare that are listed in these verses do you feel the most confident with? Which of these weapons of spiritual warfare do you believe you need to be more familiar with?

CHAPTER 19

THE DEVIL
NEVER KICKS
A DEAD HORSE

Matthew 5:11-12

"Blessed are you when others revile you and persecute you and utter all kinds of evil against you falsely on my account. Rejoice and be glad, for your reward is great in heaven, for so they persecuted the prophets who were before you." (ESV)

1 Peter 3:13 -17

Now who is there to harm you if you are zealous for what is good? But even if you should suffer for righteousness' sake, you will be blessed. Have no fear of them, nor be troubled, but in your hearts honor Christ the Lord as holy, always being prepared to make a defense to anyone who asks you for a reason for the hope that is in you; yet do it with gentleness and respect, having a good

conscience, so that, when you are slandered, those who revile your
good behavior in Christ may be put to shame. For it is better to
suffer for doing good, if that should be God's will,
than for doing evil. (ESV)

This chapter is written in chronological order to show the realness of the fact that the Devil *does* kick a *living* horse. I have had many battles in the ministry just in my short time of doing ministry. I remember hearing that quote from D.L. Moody and thinking about it during many sermons that I have heard preached. My pastor, Eddie Bumpers, will say "you think the Devil is cheering us on as we move forward in ministry?" I never felt the power of the enemy so strong as I did when we started our third Discipleship House. Everything was going great for us as we were moving forward with the housing ministry. Lives were being changed, God was pouring out His blessing on us. We had great victories and all of a sudden out of nowhere the emails began to come.

I will never forget the place I was at when I got the first email from the neighbor. I had been asked to preach in a church in the little town of Ash Grove, Missouri. My friend Kevin Baker was the pastor and his father was deathly ill, and he had to take off to visit him. I love to preach so with just hours notice I was preparing and getting ready to go. I was sitting in my car and checked my emails in the driveway while I waited for a couple of our disciples to get into the car so we could leave. The emails were from the neighbor and they were vicious. This lady threatened to ruin me personally. She said "I am making you my number one enemy! How dare you move into our neighborhood with these kinds of people. I am going to make it my life's goal to ruin your funding! I am going to hold press conferences in the front yard of your house! Today I am your enemy but tomorrow there will be a thousand women just like me."

I sent her an email that read something like this "Ma'am your neighborhood is safer because our men live in it." She responded with many more threats and promises to ruin me personally. I remember one thing she said "Our neighborhood doesn't want you here!" This lady was a self-proclaimed Christian who never had the common decency to call or talk in person with any of us at Freeway Ministries. Her aim was to ruin my reputation. I will never forget the fear that I allowed to overtake me through this situation.

Anyone with access to the web could dig up my past. I do not promote sin, drugs, wickedness, or crime, but that is my testimony as a lost man. This lady continued relentlessly assaulting me through emails. That night I preached a sermon I had prepared beforehand on the Sovereignty of God. I preached on Joseph and how God used the evil done against him for his good and God's glory. That night I realized that God had me preaching to myself. Do you know what the hardest part of this whole thing was? The very next day I was to leave and preach a five day youth camp in the middle of nowhere. I was headed to Cabool, Missouri to a place called Beth Eden Bible Camp. You say, "What is so bad about that?"

There is no internet or phone service at Beth Eden. I couldn't call for help and I couldn't defend myself for five days.

God placed me in a position where I had to trust in Him alone. I will not lie to you. I found a couple spots where I could stand in a position and get a signal, but it was a faint signal. I would have to dive a mile up a rocky gravel driveway to get a faint signal and then I could get incoming emails, but could not use my phone. It was one of those things that probably took a year or two off my life. I had messages from partnered churches and businesses letting me know about this lady. She was doing her best to make good on her promise. I was waiting for someone to call with a message like "I just wanted you to know that there is a press conference with some angry neighbor in the front yard of one of your properties."

When I did check my emails, I started receiving pictures of all the businesses that supported the ministry. Then more encouragement like, "I have lots of time on my hands to ruin you." She was horrible, and the enemy was using this woman to stress me out. I had all kinds of thoughts running through my head. God had a plan that was greater than my plan and higher than my ways. Close to the end of the youth camp, I started seeing messages from other neighbors who were now concerned about their neighborhood. This woman now had her husband with her passing flyers out through the neighborhood. I had people calling me about their elderly parents and grandparents that lived in the neighborhood. The callers where upset because we had "those kind of people" in our house so close to their family members. This woman was making us out to be some kind of terrorist group.

Then I missed a call from a lady who seemed to have a tender sprit. I drove out of the camp close to the end of our stay to return my calls for the week. This lady was in charge of their secret Facebook group organized with the sole purpose to shut Freeway Ministries down. She was the administrator of the group and she happened to be a believer. I talked with her and prayed with her. We had a good talk concerning what we did at Freeway Ministries. I sent her the emails from the woman next door and she was blown away.

By the end of the camp this lady shut down the group and was a Freeway supporter. She sent me the message that she sent the group and it was very encouraging to me. The message said, "I am a Christian and under my Christian conviction I can no longer be a part of what you all are doing to Freeway Ministries. I have checked the credibility of this organization with the local churches and they all speak highly of John Stroup and Freeway Ministries. You can either have someone else be the administrator of the group or I am shutting it down."

Weeks later, I received a call from the Greene County Commissioners telling me that there was a group of over twenty families that demanded a meeting at City Hall. He met with them, at a local church of all places. He told me that he thought I was in danger and that our men needed to be careful around the house they were staying in. He told me that he had to throw a couple of the men out of the meeting because they were out of control. I thought, "What in the world? They might as well grab the pitchforks and torches." Not too long after that, the lady emailed me again and said, "I have done all I can. I see there is nothing I can do, you win! You leave me alone and I will leave you alone." God won that victory and He did it without me lifting one finger.

Sometimes God will put you in a position that is vulnerable, so you can see how powerful He is. God wanted me to wait on Him and be still! Reminds me of the verse in Psalm 46:10 "Be still and know that I am God. I will be exalted among the nations, I will be exalted in the earth!" (ESV) One of the things that I have learned through the housing ministry is that people fear what they don't understand. To date, we have never had the police come to our house with any issues concerning behavior of any kind because of our people. We have never had one person get a charge while living at one of our houses under our leadership. We have never had a fist fight break out at one of our houses, not even once. We make our communities safer, and break the criminal mentality of our men and women.

These people who were so concerned about "these types of people in their neighborhood" were the ones acting like criminals. What if the people in your home lived by the same structure that our houses had to follow? You must attend church, zero tolerance for drugs or alcohol, no threats of violence, no filthy language, no inappropriate joking, no romantic relationships, everyone must be involved in discipleship, and house meetings three times a week. They must give back to serve the community every week. We invite the community to join our meetings and have an open-door policy for anyone who wants to take a tour. Could you handle that structure? See that is what we are about. That is what makes it so special. We are doing everything we can to live above reproach! We want to make an impact on those around us for Christ. I will continue to share how the enemy has fought against what God was doing in my life and the lives of those effected by the ministry of Freeway.

REFLECTIONS AND DISCIPLESHIP

Scripture teaches clearly that Satan has a three-point plan for your life. Satan desires only to kill, steal, and destroy. But Christ came that you might have abundant life (John 10:10). When an individual is striving to make a difference for the kingdom they will face serious opposition. Unfortunately, there are times when we allow this opposition to cause great anxiety in our lives. The Apostle Paul declares "Do not be anxious about anything, but in everything by prayer and supplication with thanksgiving let your requests be made known to God. And the peace of God, which surpasses all understanding, will guard your hearts and your minds in Christ Jesus" (Philippians 4:6-7, ESV). When you are under serious assaults from Satan, you should remember that the Lord has already won the battle (Romans 8:37-39; 2 Chronicles 20:15), and that you should not be anxious.

Discussion Questions

Use these questions in a small group or discipleship setting. Answer your questions in a notebook following the reading of this chapter.

1. Have there been times in your life when individuals have threatened to make assaults on your character and ministry? How did you respond to this situation? If you have not had this occur, then how do you plan on responding to a situation like the one mentioned above?

2. Pastor Eddie Bumpers will often ask "[Do] you think the Devil is cheering us on as we move forward in ministry?" How do you respond to the idea that you have a spiritual enemy who is after you? What are you doing to engage in proper spiritual warfare?

3. In this chapter the author noted that he felt helpless in many ways regarding to how he was to respond. Look up the following passages of Scripture: Isaiah 26:3; Psalm 119:165; Isaiah 41:10. How do these passages inform you about fear and uncertainty?

4. When you face uncertainty or anxiety causing situations, would having passages like the ones listed above memorized be helpful, how so?

REFERENCES

1. D. L. Moody

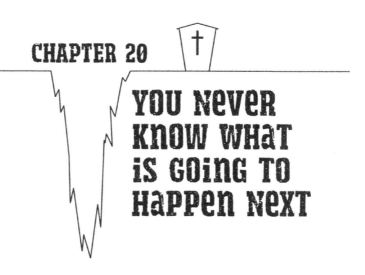

CHAPTER 20

YOU NEVER KNOW WHAT IS GOING TO HAPPEN NEXT

Proverbs 3:5-6
Trust in the LORD with all your heart, and do not lean on your
own understanding. In all your ways acknowledge Him, and He
will make straight your paths. (ESV)

Romans 11:33
Oh, the depth of the riches and wisdom and knowledge of God!
How unsearchable are His judgments and how inscrutable His
ways! (ESV)

If I was to ask you to describe your Christian walk in one word, what would your word be? Think about that question for a moment. Look deep into the Scriptures and see those people who God used in a mighty way, and describe their lives in one word. Would it be the same as yours? Hebrews 11 is full of people who changed the world through faith and obedience through following the God of the Bible. If we're all going to be honest, that question is a scary one to ask. The one word to describe my Christian walk would be *adventure*. This whole book is described as my journey; you could say, "My adventure from the pit to the pulpit." The stories I've been telling you are a part of that adventure, or to keep the theme of the book, *journey*. There are some things that we expect God to do and then some things that He does that we never see coming. This chapter is dedicated to one of those things.

In 2012 I was preaching a youth camp at Crossway Baptist Church, in Springfield, Missouri. It was my first time preaching at Crossway and I was stoked to bring the message that night. The was a message titled, *Pick Up the Ball*. I have no clue what the sermon was about but I clearly remember the title. After the sermon was over I was in the gym eating and had one of the many youth pastors there ask me if I would be interested in preaching at a Jubilee at their church that next year. I agreed to come, if they would have me, and that was the end of the conversation.

The next year I got a card from Mt. Vernon, Illinois. I opened it up, and lo and behold, it was an invite to the Jubilee. I had no clue how many times I would be asked to preach at this event and they were kind of secretive about it as well. This was what the brothers down south call a *camp meeting*. I built three sermons to preach for this event. Then the day came for my wife and I to head from Springfield, Missouri to Mt. Vernon, Illinois. I remember it was a torrential down pour as we drove. This was one of the first times I was asked to go and preach at a church. I was excited, nervous, insecure, and didn't know what to expect.

I did not know anyone at the place I was going. The young preacher who invited me was someone I had met one time. I remember it was raining so bad that I could hardly see to drive. After we arrived at the hotel, I had to run everything upstairs to our room, and then we had a few minutes to leave for the first night of this camp meeting. I shared the elevator with a gentleman who was staring me up and down. So I shared Christ with him, because I thought, "If anyone needs Jesus, it is this guy!"

I shared that I used to be a bad guy and the Lord saved me in an old dirty prison cell. I also told this fella that God had called me into the ministry. Then I shared how I was there to preach a youth conference. He looked at me and said, "Youth conference? I am pretty sure that there is no youth conference going on around here." The puzzled look on his face made me worry a bit. I had prepared three youth messages and of course youth messages are directed toward the youth. Things like "listen to your parents and things about school." I got to the little church in the middle of nowhere and the first thing I asked was, "Where are the kids?" The lady said, "Kids? There are no kids here. This is a Jubilee for preachers and those in ministry to refresh each other."

I wish you could have seen the look on my face when the lady said those words. I thought, "Oh no! How can I preach these messages to preachers that are directed toward youth?" I thought, "Great I am about to preach a messages about *listening to your parents* and *temptations at school* to a bunch of preachers." I was sweating it and praying! I wanted to fake a heart attack and get back to my hotel room! I just needed some time to change my messages a bit. Then I met the minister who was heading up this event. He came to me and said, "Here at the Jubilee you need to be ready to preach because you never know when you will be called." I thought, "What in the world?" I was silently praying that God would let me escape to the hotel and fix my messages.

After we ate, everyone went into the sanctuary to have a seat and see who would be the first preacher. After the introduction, Pastor Tim called the first preacher, and he preached the paint off the walls. He was an old timer named John Smith, and I honestly felt intimidated. Then they called the second preacher. He was the fella I met in the elevator! That guy who I thought needed Jesus was David Gidcumb, and he also was an outstanding preacher (do not tell him I said that). When they gave us our schedule and sent us back to the hotel I felt like building an altar and calling on the name of the Lord for His grace. I was ready to go Old Testament!

I got back to the hotel and told Sharla what was going on, and she laughed at me. She said, "What are you going to do now?" Sharla is good at encouraging me through difficult times like this. I spent half the night changing some of the wording, praying, meditating, and could not hardly sleep, due to who was in attendance at the Jubilee. I was called to preach with some of the best preachers I had ever heard! I was not even ordained or licensed to preach!

The next morning we woke up and drove to the church for breakfast. I had gone over my notes a hundred times. We were called into the sanctuary and the first preacher was called and then the second preacher. Then we had lunch and Pastor Jared Bumpers came up to me during lunch. He was the only person that I knew there, and I was thankful for a familiar face. He said "John, if they ask you to preach after lunch you better bring the heat." He said "Everyone is going to be full, and trying to go to sleep." Guess who they called after lunch? Give up yet? Yea that's right, they called my name. I thought, "Man, here we go!"

I preached my heart out and at the end of the message the pastor came to the front of the church. He said, "I do not know what to do at a time like this." It was quiet as a mouse. God was working in the crowd and I believe that conviction was on the hearts of those listening. Then all of a sudden out of the crowd of that little country church an old man jumped up and hollered, "AMEN! Praise the Lord for what He has done in that young man's life! Let him preach another one!" Then Pastor Tim looked at me and said, "Do you have another message?"

I will never forget the look on the face of my friend, Pastor Jared Bumpers. He was the same guy who told me to bring the heat if they called me after lunch. He just sank down in his seat and gave me a look like, *better you then me buddy*! I preached another sermon and things went well for us there. We experienced a real move of God in our marriage through that meeting! We needed it because at that time in our ministry we were hurting bad. God used that camp meeting to grow and strengthen us as a couple. I learned a couple things from that camp meeting. The first thing I learned was that I preach the same to the youth as I do to the grownups. Then I learned that you never know what God is going to do through the doors that He opens for you.

I preached the last sermon of the meeting. I was the only preacher to preach three times and I had prepared three sermons. I wonder what would have happened if I had prepared four sermons? Through that meeting I gained some good friends and have preached for three of them on a regular basis. Two of the pastors lead churches that support our ministry. That crazy looking dude I met in the elevator that day is the guy who sent my wife and I to Africa. God has a sense of humor but always uses it for our good and His glory, if we will just walk through those doors that He opens!

REFLECTIONS AND DISCIPLESHIP

You never know what opportunities await those who will diligently seek to follow the Lord. The Lord has a plan that will work ultimately to bring Him glory (Ephesians 1:11). The Lord brings people into our path and opens doors when we don't know what He is doing. We are called, however, to strain towards the goal that Christ has set before us. That is the goal of the "upward call of God in Jesus" (Philippians 3:14). Our faith and seeking after the Lord is a race and a journey we must diligently commit to.

DISCUSSION QUESTIONS

Use these questions in a small group or discipleship setting. Answer your questions in a notebook following the reading of this chapter.

1. Who are some individuals that the Lord has put in your path to encourage you and to serve beside you?

2. What are you doing to make the most of the opportunities that Christ has given you?

3. Read Philippians 3:12-14. When you reflect on your personal journey of faith, what have been some key times when the Lord has shown up and put you in the right place at the right time?

4. What are you doing at this time to press on towards your faith and to forget the failings from the past that lay behind you?

5. Who are some individuals that you are currently encouraging as they strain forward in their personal faith journey? How are you encouraging them?

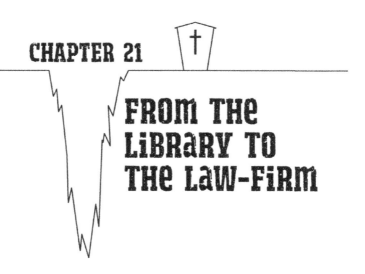

CHAPTER 21

FROM THE LIBRARY TO THE LAW-FIRM

Ephesians 3:20

Now to Him who is able to do far more abundantly than all that we ask or think, according to the power at work within us, (ESV)

1 Corinthians 2:9

But, as it is written, "What no eye has seen, nor ear heard, nor the heart of man imagined, what God has prepared for those who love Him" (ESV)

Do you ever sit back and look at what God has done and think to yourself, "Man, I never saw that coming!" I can sit here in my office and know without a doubt that it is only a miracle that I am where I am! God almighty, the God of all glory, has placed me here. Some days it is hard, even for me, to believe all that God has done.

I met a man who was formerly a pastor named Shannon. Shannon is a rough looking fella that loves to ride Harley Davidsons! He is one of a kind and serves at our Northside Freeway Ministries outreach in Springfield. Shannon is a dear friend and a great help to many in ministry. He is always working on one of our vehicles. Shannon introduced me to a lovely couple that would become like a mom and dad to me. Little did I know that my family and ministry would be forever changed after that day. I invited them to Freeway Ministries and they came. I remember when Jim Corbett came to a service, and it was clear that he was forced into it. I remember when I told him "Jim our meetings start at 6:00pm, and end at 8:00pm." He looked at me and said, "What? Are you kidding me?" Worship started, and people started filling the building. Jim and Deborah fell in love with Freeway Ministries. I began to work with a loved one that had been struggling, and our relationship grew. They honestly became like a mother and father to my wife and I.

Throughout the history of our relationship they knew I didn't have an office. My home is small so there is nowhere there to have an office. I would just leave my house in the morning and go to a coffee shop or the library. One day Jim came to me and said, "You need an office, John. Would you like to have an office in my law-firm?" I thought, "Are you kidding me?" I said sure and they agreed to put me somewhere in the building when their remodel was over.

After the remodel was over I thought, "They will probably put me somewhere hidden in the basement so no one can see me." They didn't do that at all. They placed me directly in the middle of five lawyers! Can you believe that? John Stroup, a homeless needle junkie, convicted crack dealer, who just years ago was living in a shelter, now sitting in his own office between five lawyers. I think that the Lord is laughing at all of this. Before this happened, I can see God sitting in heaven saying, "Wait for it, wait for it, and now look at his face! Did you see the look on his face? Hey, John I bet you never saw that coming!"

I cannot begin to describe the love and generosity that this family has shown us! Jim and Deborah are a vital part of our Midtown Freeway. We planted a Freeway Ministries alongside their church First Baptist, Springfield, Missouri. They meet every Friday night and they serve food. They also prepare meals there. As of now, there has been a Freeway Ministries outreach at that church for over three years. They also approached us about a property in Marshfield that is on a lake and bigger than two of our houses combined. We call it *The Ranch*. There is currently seventeen men on the ranch, a screen printing business, and a small cattle operation.

When I was in prison I had no clue what the Lord was going to do with my life! I can promise you that I didn't see this coming! I want those reading this book to understand that the results of your life are in God's hands. I can guarantee, without a shadow of a doubt, that those who chase after God's heart will be shocked at the things He can and will do with your life. Warren Wiersbe put it best "God gives His best to those who leave the choice up to Him." Think about David as a shepherd boy rejected by his family, and one day the God of the universe would make him His king. I cannot imagine how David felt leading his people after being counted out, and rejected his whole life, but I can sure relate.

Many people gave up on me, and some today are waiting for me to fall. I know that it is God who orchestrates things like this to happen. God is in the middle of this and no one can stop God. God has used people like Jim and his wife Deborah as a surrogate family for me. When I need counsel or someone to talk with, I have family that will be there at the drop of a hat. There have been many things that have separated me from being as close as I would like to with my biological family. But through Christ, I now have people that are there in a heartbeat.

I thank God for all of the people that He has put in my life! Jim and Deborah have been very generous and kind in more ways than I can share. Every time I walk into the office, pull up my shades, and look out my window I think to myself, "Only God could have done something like this." You must understand the situation I am in. It is so hard many times to express in words how I feel. I was a homeless junkie, family was dead or in prison, lost, and nowhere to turn, and then saved by grace in a prison cell just ten years ago. I haven't even been out of prison for very long. I was homeless not that long ago without a clue of what was going to happen with my life.

I can assure you that this was not in the plans that I had; but God's plan is another story. Now I am sitting in a law-firm, trusted by the owners, taken care of in every way, married to a wonderful wife, a father, directing a non-profit ministry, and about to start another one in South Africa! How does that happen? If your reading this and you doubt the power of Jesus Christ, then read this chapter over and look at what He can do! You need to reach out to Him in prayer and be committed to whatever He puts in front of you! If He can do it for me He can do it for anyone! God definitely has a sense of humor.

REFLECTIONS AND DISCIPLESHIP

Proverbs 16:9 says, "The heart of man plans his way, but the Lord establishes his steps." (ESV) It is evident that the Lord will work in the lives of those who will simply trust His leading. Scripture over and over demonstrates that God often uses the outcast. 1 Samuel 16:7 states that the Lord sees the heart of a man and does not consider his appearance. The Lord knows very clearly the plans He has to use those who will repent of their sins and trust him with their future. In fact, the Lord knows the history of your future.

DISCUSSION QUESTIONS

Use these questions in a small group or discipleship setting. Answer your questions in a notebook following the reading of this chapter.

1. Read John 1:43-51. In Nathaniel's initial encounter with Christ, it was evident that Jesus saw who Nathaniel would be. When you consider that the Lord knows who He is creating you to be, how does this make you feel, and how does this challenge you to seek him at a deeper level?

2. In this chapter the author shared how the Lord changed the initial responses that some had when they first encountered the work of Freeway Ministries. Has there been a time when the Lord used you to initiate a change or a softening of the heart in another individual? What was that experience like?

3. In this chapter the author expressed that there have been a few *only God could have done that* moments. When you think back to the way the Lord has directed your life, what *only God could have done that* moments have you had?

4. The author expressed in this chapter that there are still some individuals who are waiting to see him fall. How

do you deal with those individuals who seem to be only waiting for your failure? What can you do to ensure that you do not fall?

References

1. Wiersbe, Warren W. On Being a Leader for God. Baker Books, 2011.

CHAPTER 22

THE MOST DANGEROUS PLACE YOU CAN BE IS CLOSE TO JESUS

2 Timothy 3:12
Indeed, all who desire to live a godly life in Christ Jesus will be
persecuted (ESV)

Luke 22:12
Then Satan entered into Judas called Iscariot, who was of the
number of the twelve. (ESV)

2 Corinthians 12:7
I was given a thorn in my flesh, a messenger of Satan to buffet
me... (ESV)

Many times those who follow Christ forget the dangerous parts of it. Understand that the community I serve sends the worst-case scenarios to Freeway Ministries. If someone has a loved one, a neighbor, a co-worker, or homeless person that they cannot reach, then many times I get the phone calls. I will say many times, and I want you to put this word in your hearts for me: "MINISTRY IS MESSY! IF YOU DO NOT GET MESSY THEN YOU ARE NOT DOING MINISTRY!"

Where do you think the most dangerous place for a believer to be is, in all reality? It is close to Jesus! That is where you are the biggest threat to the enemy! Now I know what many may be thinking. You may say, "I am always close to Jesus because He is in me and I am in Him." Maybe you're saying, "The Lord protects me, and nothing can happen to me unless He allows it." I would agree 100% with those statements!

What about Peter, Paul, and all the Apostles? What happened to them? Where was Judas when Satan entered his heart? He was right next to Jesus! How about the time when Jesus told Peter that Satan was asking for him? Have you ever thought about that? Sit down and think about that statement for one minute! The most powerful, evil force in the universe is desiring you; the evil of all evil knows your name and wants to *sift you as wheat*. Have you ever sifted something? It is a process of shaking, and sorting things out. I think that Satan wanted to sift the faith out of Peter because Jesus said "Simon, Simon (Peter's other name), Satan demanded to have you that he might sift you like wheat, but I have prayed for you, Simon, that your faith may not fail…" (See Luke 22:31-32, ESV). I believe with all my heart, like Job, Peter, Daniel and many others in the Bible we are under greater pressure from Satan the closer we are to Jesus. The enemy wants to sift us, and desires to drain us of faith. Remember when those Jews tried to cast out those demons like Paul but didn't know Jesus personally?

Acts 19:13-15
Then some of the itinerant Jewish exorcists undertook to invoke the name of the Lord Jesus over those who had evil spirits, saying, "I adjure you by the Jesus whom Paul proclaims." Seven sons of a Jewish high priest named Sceva were doing this. But the evil spirit answered them, "Jesus I know, and Paul I recognize, but who are you?" (ESV)

What about Job? Job was a man who loved the Lord, was up right, and even made offerings to God just in case his children were out of line! What did that do for Job? It put a target on him and once again Satan desired him! He was in a dangerous place by being close to the Lord! I think I have made my point.

When You are close to God, serving God, loving God, and doing *all the right things* expect hardship. Expect God to allow you to suffer in His perfect will. See that is Biblical Christianity 101! Those who are close to the Lord will suffer. It is not *if you suffer*, but *when you suffer*. I have found that those trials bring out the best and the worst in us. Throughout those trials we are changed and grow closer to the Lord than we have ever been before. I would encourage you to take the time to study the Scriptures that promise hardship and suffering. How many verses do you have on your heart? Think of your favorite memory verse. Is it one that promises suffering and the blessing that come from it? Honestly, I never thought about that until pain, fear, threats, and conflict came my way from doing the right thing. Then I studied suffering, persecution and the blessings that come from them.

These stories I am going to share from my journey are not in chronological order, but they are 100% fact. I hope that you are blessed, encouraged, and strengthened from them. I enjoy what Elisabeth Elliot said about suffering. Her husband was killed while trying to reach a people group for the Lord. Jim Elliot was a man of God who died a martyr's death from being close to Jesus. Elizabeth Elliot stated: "I am not a theologian or a scholar, but I am very aware of the fact that pain is necessary to all of us. In my own life, I think I can honestly say that out of the deepest pain has come the strongest conviction of the presence of God and the love of God."[1]

VIRGIL AND THE SHANK[2]

When we started our second Freeway Ministries location in the worst neighborhood in Springfield, Missouri, I met this man named Virgil. The way we met is not the way you meet most people in ministry. The model for starting a Freeway Ministries outreach is very simple but effective. We go throughout the neighborhood knocking on doors walking up and down the street as we hand out flyers. We invite people to come. We have food, fellowship, music, childcare, and the life-changing message of hope in Christ.

Well, our first night Rick Lechner decided to invite the homeless guy who slept in the bushes of the church, inside to eat and hear the message. His name was Virgil, and he was very aggressive. When Rick woke him up and asked him if he would like to come inside to eat and hear the good news of Jesus Christ, he pulled out a giant knife on Rick! He said, "I will stab you!" That was our first official introduction to Mr. Virgil. He ended up coming quite regularly, and caused problems all the time. You must understand that Freeway Ministries allows certain things to go on that most churches won't. We want people to hear the Gospel, and as long as they listen and behave, they can stay. Virgil would dance around like a kick boxer while you were talking to him. He is close to six foot, six inches tall and dances like Bruce Lee when he is in a street fight. As funny as that sounds, it is a bit nerve racking. He also would talk to himself and just bust out laughing right in the middle of the message. Try preaching through that.

Well, he continued to cause issues and one night we had enough. He was hiding in the bathroom after Freeway was over and the security team found him. They had to ask him to leave, and after much disrespectful behavior, Virgil left the building. I told the security team not to let him come back inside, but that he could have a to-go plate of food anytime he was hungry. I was the donation pick-up man and everything else you could imagine when Freeway first started. One day I was taking my little boy to the Discovery Center with a friend and his son. They had met us there. I had tons of donated bread and different things in the van with me. I had to stop by the church, and drop the food after we finished. My friend said "John, why don't you let me take Keith with me while you go and do that?" So, I went on my way and pulled into the church parking lot.

I parked in the back of the church off the street. The back of the church was secluded and out of sight. No one was at the church but me. I walked around the van and started unpacking it. Then as soon as I turned around guess who was standing there dancing like Bruce Lee? Virgil was red in the face and very unhappy. I thought, "Oh boy, I didn't see him coming!" While standing there with my hands full of boxes of donated food, I said, "What can I do for you?" In those short moments I was working the situation out in my head, and running different scenarios through while he was doing his preparation to attack. Then he spoke "I heard that you didn't want me here anymore." Trying to buy some time I asked "Who told you that?" It was me and the crazy guy who lived in the bushes who was known to carry a shank. Both of my hands were full of bread boxes. What would you have done?

I will be as honest as I can be here. I was caught off guard and surprised by this six-foot plus tall bush man who was very unhappy with me. What he said next left me speechless. He said, "The security team told me you said I couldn't come back." I thought to myself, "Way to go security! Boy, you did a great job of protecting the preacher on this one. They dropped the dime on me." Then, all of a sudden I was at peace and said "Yes sir, you are right I did say it. Virgil, you are always causing issues and creating a hostile environment for us." Then I said, "Well go ahead and hit me." I have no clue why I said those words, but I did. He just looked at me. Then again I said, "Well, are you going to hit me? I did tell them that. You cannot behave yourself, so you cannot come anymore Virgil." He just stopped and looked at me. He said, "You ain't worth my time." He started cursing me out and walking off.

As soon as he got around the building I called 911 because I thought "He is going to the bushes to get his shank." Then as I spoke with the operator I could tell he was not going to attack me because the curse words were getting farther and farther away. I would see Virgil from time to time, but to this day, I haven't been in another similar situation again with him. Let me share some insight with you from this story. God protected me during this time. Remember that my friend asked to take my little boy with him right before I delivered that bread? The Lord protected my son who was still in preschool at the time. I do not think I would have been as passive if I would have had my little boy with me. I thank God for His sovereignty. I can look back and see His hand over my life. Praise the Lord.

There are always ramifications to situations like this one though. You think about all the *what if's* after it is all said and done. Then I have to tell my wife to be careful when she is out because people recognize my family. I think about her and my kids during seasons like this one. Knowing that people who want to harm me could do more damage by harming my family. Then she worries about me as well while I am out doing ministry. Remember being close to Jesus is a dangerous place to be.

THE ABUSIVE EX-HUSBAND

In 2011, when we started our first Freeway Ministries outreach we were at Broadway Baptist Church. We had a Sunday School class that met off site, a little over a city block away from the church. We had a couple from the church ask us to reach out to their daughter. She was a drug addict with two little kids. This is not an uncommon situation for us. Churches all over the United States are full of parents like the ones I just mentioned.

Her name was Jessica and you could tell she had been abused. One of our leaders reached out to her and she came to Freeway Ministries on a Saturday night and gave her life to Jesus. She had two amazing little ones: a boy and a girl. She began to attend the Freeway Sunday School class and would always ask for prayer concerning her husband in prison. He was soon to get out and she was very concerned about what he was going to do when he came home. She wanted him to come to church and be a real husband. She wanted what most women want: someone to love them, someone to provide, protect, and be a part of their children's lives.

Her dad was very concerned about the release of this guy, due to his past. She was doing so good for herself. The day finally came that everyone was concerned about, and we only saw Jessica once more after her husband was released. No one heard any more out of this young lady and we all knew what had happened to her. One of the saddest parts of the ministry is losing people. Everyone's fears had come true. She went back to her old life when he was released from prison.

Next, something happened that no one could have prepared for. Julie and Mike, two of our leaders, received an unexpected phone call one afternoon from Jessica. She was crying and upset. She was distraught and afraid as well. She called Julie for help. Julie, along with Mike, picked her up from a park; more like rescued her from a park. This whole event, to this day, is one of the greatest examples of true Christianity I have ever seen in my life. Mike and Julie not only rescued Jessica, but God used them to change the course of generations to come, starting with Jessica's children.

Jessica wasn't the same old punching bag that she had always been before. Her husband was driving with her *while* he was beating on her, and she wanted out. She asked him to let her out of the car, but he would not. She jumped out of the car and ran from him. She made it to a local park in Springfield before he caught her. He began to beat her and bash her head into a bench. There were some men playing basketball at the park that day who saw what was happening, and jumped in and fought him off.

She called Julie, and they came to pick her up. They took her to the husband's parents' house to pick up her two kids. Then they did something that most people would never dream of doing. They moved her and her two kids into their home. They protected her, and we came alongside her. She pressed charges on this man and got an order of protection. This was not the first time he beat her up, but it would be the last. He went to prison and she divorced him. Jessica was learning everything for the first time. She was learning how to raise her kids; two kids who had no structure and were as wild as you could imagine. Mike and Julie really ministered to this family in a way that makes a person proud to know them. They would have to hold these two kids down sometimes due to the rage inside of them. They had to walk through life with Jessica to help her learn how to parent and discipline her children as well.

Over a year went by, and Jessica met a man named Casey in the ministry. Casey was a guy just starting his life over as well. He was living in a transitional living environment and came to Freeway Ministries by getting on the wrong bus. Casey thought he was going to another church and ended up at Freeway before he knew what happened. Casey was a man who had been to prison, strung out on drugs, burned many bridges in his life, and failed his whole life at being responsible.

Casey had a very rough past, and was raised without a mother or a father. His mother was a drug addict and he had an impossible childhood. He had a fire in his heart for the Lord and was as serious as one might imagine. Casey finally had enough of the criminal life and was tired of failing. Casey became very involved in Freeway

Casey serving with his kids.

Ministries. He was winning people to the Lord, and would invite everyone in the half-way house to come every chance he got. During that year, with Jessica being at Freeway and involved in one of our local churches, they became fond of each other.

Casey approached Mike and Julie to ask for permission to date Jessica. We were all very concerned about this but allowed it to happen with strict guide lines. We were, and still are, protective over our people. Casey was very submissive, humble, and respectful while he courted Jessica. Jessica is like a daughter to me and her children are precious as well. Today, I look back at this and honestly I am very proud of the way they courted, and the way they handled themselves. Remember, Jessica had so much baggage hanging over her head. Two kids that were very rebellious and a psychotic ex-husband that was going to be released from prison soon. Casey was not without his fair share of baggage as well. He was also divorced and had two girls he failed from the past.

Casey, Jessica, and their kids.

I had the privilege and honor to marry these two. Casey and Jessica became a great team; working together to reach people with the Gospel of Jesus Christ. They had many struggles, but overcame them by the blood of Jesus. You can find them at Freeway Ministries every Saturday night faithfully serving and leading people to the Lord. Casey has been a great example to Jessica's two kids, and Jessica has been there for Casey's two daughters.

One day I was pulling into the parking lot on a Saturday afternoon, and while walking across the parking lot I noticed a struggle by the front door. It was more than a struggle it was a fight. Anyone who has been in the streets knows when they see a fight. I noticed the scuffle out of the corner of my eye. I said, "Hey! Stop right now!" Then I saw the one guy pull out a gun and I heard him say, "I will kill you." He backed up and jumped in a car with the gun pointed at our security team. I was waiting for the gunshots as the car peeled out of the parking lot.

It was Jessica's ex-husband. Mike was there an hour early and saw this guy in the building. Mike is the one who took Jessica in his house. He yelled at the fella. He told him he was not allowed in the building and that he wasn't supposed to be there. The guy punched Mike in the face and the fight was on. The guy must not have known that Mike was a trained MMA fighter. Mike wrapped him up in some sort of hold until one of our security guys pulled Mike off him to get the guy out of the door. That is when he pulled out the gun.

I cannot tell you how blessed we are that no one got hurt. The police could not find this guy and everyone was concerned about Jessica and Casey. We were all on high alert. This went on for months and no one knew what would happen next. Jessica and Casey grew in the Lord through this situation, and we all learned how to trust God a lot more as well. Let me share with you the amazing things that happened because of this scary ordeal.

We learned a lesson in the sovereignty of God. Remember when I said that Jessica and Casey never missed Freeway on Saturday night? Well, that Saturday night they planned to be out of town. The night this guy planned on sneaking into the building with a gun was one of the rare nights that they were going to be gone. To this day, we are not sure what her ex-husband would have done or what his plans were if they would have been there. God, in His grace and wisdom, took care of them.

The news team from KOLR 10 news in Springfield got wind of the story and wanted to interview us about it. They came and asked us some questions concerning this guy and about salvation in Christ. The reporter asked me, "Do you think a guy like that can be saved?" I said, "I used to be that guy. Yes, he can be saved, and that is why we do what we do." I shared the Gospel and they did not edit it at all. What a testimony of God's power and grace. Remember, we see things from a set of earthly lenses, but God always has a plan. His ways are not our ways. The story could be finished but there is much more to this story.

The children are not the only people who are innocent victims in these types of situations. Many times, there are also grandparents, aunts, uncles, and family members that are caught in the crossfire as well. In this case there were two very caring and wonderful grandparents on the ex-husbands side of the family. These two grandparents were a big part of Jessica's children's lives. When a man is running lose with a gun, making threats, and highly dangerous, precautions must be made.

Casey and Jessica called the grandparents. They told them that they wanted them to be a part of the kid's lives but they couldn't leave them at their house anymore due to the danger of this man running lose. Casey told the grandpa, J.R., "We want you to be a part of our family, and not just physically but spiritually as well. Come to church and visit the kids. Come to Freeway Ministries and visit the kids." Do you know what happened next? They got close to the Lord and joined the church. They are now a part of our family and a part of the very outreach that their son brought a gun to. They both serve every Saturday night, and it is not because that is the only place they can see the kids. Their son has been in prison for a couple years now and they are still faithful. J.R.

works security and Debby works in the childcare. How amazing is that?

You cannot make that kind of stuff up. God worked through that horrible situation to bring about His glory and honor. If that crazed ex-husband would not have brought that gun who knows what would have happened in the lives of the grandparents. Because of that bad situation so many awesome things have happened. Today, Casey and Jessica have a baby of their own named Myah. My wife and I have babysat this little girl since she was six weeks old and she is one of many Freeway babies. They are all my spiritual grandchildren and my life would not be the same without them.

Myah is going on three years old now. The other two children Blayden and Alissa, their other kids are both saved. These two kids are bright and being raised in the church house instead of the dope house. This is one of the many reasons why we do Freeway Ministries. Just think of where these kids would be today if it wasn't for the Lord intervening into their lives like He did. Remember, the most dangerous place to be is close to Jesus.

THE MONGREL

In 2016 I began to preach revival for a Pastor in Cape Town, South Africa. If you know anything about South Africa you know that it is one of the most dangerous countries in the world. The area that I had been called to evangelize in is the western area of Cape Town, South Africa called Lavender Hill. I met the Pastor of Lakeview Community Church through David Gidcumb, the fella I mentioned earlier in the book that I met on the elevator in Mt. Vernon, Illinois.

David's church supports Lakeview Community Church on a monthly basis. David had mentioned my name to Gerald November, the pastor of that church. David flew Gerald and his wife Mrs. Desiree to the USA for a get away from ministry. They came to Freeway Ministries and ask me to come and preach for their church. They needed an evangelist to come. Their church was full of ex-gangsters and addicts. They have a special church in the middle of a very

rough area in Cape Town. I learned about the different gangs in Cape Town. One of the oldest gangs is called the Mongrel gang. If you look up the most dangerous prisoner in the world you will find a

John and Sharla at Lavender Hill, Cape Town, South Africa.

prisoner named John Mongrel who ran the Mongrel gang.

Well John Mongrel had a protégé who I will not mention by name but I will call him Ron. Pastor Gerald had been going to Ron's compound to meet with him for a while. Ron was very dangerous and Gerald's wife would get upset when he went to meet with Ron. Ron's body guards, who were all high on meth would allow Pastor Gerald to enter and share the Gospel with Ron. See, Ron could not leave the flat he lived in because the rival gangs would kill him the moment he left.

Pastor Gerald asked me the second year I preached in Cape Town if I would go with him to meet with Ron. I thought, "Man what are you getting me into." I knew that there were at least three local gangs that were looking to murder this man, and that his home was shot up at least once a week. I went anyway. Here I am, the preacher from the United States walking up the stairs of this housing project in Lavender Hill to the most notorious gangster's door.

I walked into the room and he was very aggressive. You could tell he didn't know what to do when I came in. He explained that he had wanted to be a gangster his whole life and that he was trapped in his gang. While he was talking, he started speaking in prison slang to his gangster friend who was in the kitchen bagging up the meth or what they call in South Africa, *tic.* Pastor Gerald didn't even understand prison slang. As Ron explained his situation he started showing me the bullet holes through the house and told me stories of the hits that the other gangs tried to make on him. Pointing at the curtains behind my head, he said, "This is where they just tried to kill me last week." Right then I realized that I was sitting in front of the window facing the street. At the end of our visit Ron allowed me to pray for him and was receptive to the message of the cross. I took off my shirt and he seen all the tattoos on my body. He listened to me and honestly calmed down quite a bit after that. That could have been the

269

last trip for me, but God allowed me to walk away from that situation. My prayers are that God would make me more dangerous than safe. I want to make a mark on this world for Jesus and be a real threat to the plans of the enemy. Remember, being a Christian is not being safe.

Took Greg Craig to Silver Dollar City.

Introducing Greg to live turkeys.

On our way to Cape Town, South Africa!

Sharla and some of the ladies from Lakeview Community Church.

Sharla speaking at Lakeview.

Serving in one of Cape Town's many shanty towns.

John and Sharla live on Cape Town radio!

Greg Craig with Freeway Ministries van in Cape Town.

Freeway Ministries van in service in Cape Town.

REFLECTIONS AND DISCIPLESHIP

Jesus shares with His followers in Acts 1:8 that they are to share the Gospel in take it to "the end of the earth." In Mark 16:15, Jesus shares that His followers are to "proclaim the Gospel to the whole creation." In Matthew 28:19, Jesus tells the disciples to "go therefore and make disciples of all nations." When one takes the word of the Gospel to these places, Jesus and His promises must be taken with them. He shares in Matthew's Gospel that "I am with you always, to the end of the age" (Matthew 28:20, ESV). Certainly, if one is taking the words of Christ seriously they will face many hardships and many difficult situations. Jesus was very clear in noting that if He was persecuted those who chose to follow him would also be persecuted (John 15:20).

DISCUSSION QUESTIONS

Use these questions in a small group or discipleship setting. Answer your questions in a notebook following the reading of this chapter.

1. When you consider that the most dangerous place you can be is to be close to Jesus, how does this make you feel?

2. There are many who claim the name of Christ and then turn around and claim that if you are walking with Christ then everything will be just fine. As has been evidence in this book, walking with Christ does not mean everything will be easy. What are some of your most serious fears when it comes to possible hardships you may have to face as you live dangerously close to Jesus?

3. In this chapter there were three stories about God's deliverance from hardships and provision in difficult situations. Of the three stories which one spoke the most directly to you?

4. In the book of Genesis there is the story of Joseph. The story runs from Genesis 37 to Genesis 50. In the story, Joseph is betrayed by his brothers and for years faces difficult situations. He faces prison, he faces slavery, he faces false accusations. In the end, Joseph is able to

deliver his family from death. Read Genesis 50:18 – 21. In your life, how has God used evil things to bring about His glory?

References

1. https://www.whatchristianswanttoknow.com/top-15-christian-quotes-about-pain-and-suffering/#ixzz5CKh74jmW
2. A shank is a homemade knife that people in prison make to protect and attack other people with.

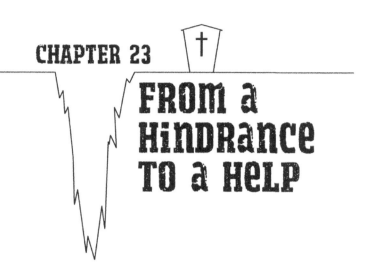

CHAPTER 23

FROM a HINDRANCE TO a HELP

Mark 5:15
And they came to Jesus and saw the demon-possessed man, the one who had had the legion, sitting there, clothed and in his right mind, and they were afraid. (ESV)

1 Timothy 1:15
The saying is trustworthy and deserving of full acceptance, that Christ Jesus came into the world to save sinners, of whom I am the foremost. (ESV)

One of the things that I struggle with is the dark things that I did in my B.C. days (Before Christ). I took so much from my community and I desire nothing more than to be able to give back. One of my hearts desires is to one day start a Freeway Ministries in my home town before I am called to glory. This would most likely be one of the most difficult things that I have ever done in my entire ministry. Regardless of the situation that a person finds themselves in it is difficult for those who you know you from the past to believe that you have been changed.

I talk with our men and women explaining this truth to them. I tell them not to be hard on those people because you honestly have to believe in the supernatural to see that it's possible for someone like us to change. To this day, many from Jefferson City, Missouri still do not believe that I am the changed man I am today. I do not blame them one bit. It is a real act of God, and without faith in a God who transforms how could a man like me change? Remember what happened to Jesus? Those from His hometown didn't believe in Him. When Jesus did things to prove who He was, He was rejected by those He knew from His past. Those from His hometown brought up His background. They said, "Isn't that the carpenter's son from Nazareth?" Look what Jesus Himself said in Mark 6:4, "A prophet is not without honor except in his hometown and among his own relatives and in his own household." (ESV) I have had so many come into the Freeway Ministries discipleship housing from my home town and only one of them have graduated so far. Some have left on their own and some have been asked to leave. I have had some that have entered the program and made it a couple weeks, and some come and make it a couple hours.

One guy came wanting to tell war stories of the past, telling the men in the house how wild I was and so on. I had to rebuke him and ask him not to glorify past sins. In the end, he ended up trying to ruin my name by making up some kind of conspiracy theory about me telling everyone that I was some kind of kingpin. I had one family from Jefferson City tell everyone that I was a double agent for the F.B.I. To be honest, I thought the F.B.I. story was kind of cool, but it is was ridiculous just the same.

I have had several from my home town come, and honestly, I have only had one person make it. One of my old friends that didn't make it ended up dying from a drug overdose. Let me share with you about the one who was successful

I received a call from a 573 area code and the caller I.D. said Jefferson City. I always think twice or wonder who it could be calling me from Jefferson City. The night the phone rang I had those feelings running through my head, "Who could that be?" I picked up the phone and it was an old running buddy from my childhood and he was crying, "Big John, is that you?" Most anyone from my past calls me Big John. This fella was broken and strung out on heroin. He was crying so bad I couldn't even understand him. It is odd because the last time I saw him we were passing each other on the prison yard and I tried to get him to go to church with me. He made fun of me and now here we are bearing the fruit of the decisions we made. I prayed with him and offered him help. I thought that God was opening a door for me to reach my childhood friend. I received a call one day from his father telling me that the police arrested him.

A few days later another call came in from a Jefferson City number. It was a girl that I didn't know, but she knew me. What I didn't know is that while I was talking to my friend, she was listening. She lived in the basement of a home with him. She got my phone number off his phone and was ready for help. This girl was in bad as shape. Her name is Hannah. I asked her "Are you willing to do whatever it takes?" She said, "Yes." I had a friend in recovery go and get her from Jefferson City and bring her to Springfield. He happened to live in Columbia, Missouri which was closer to her than I or anyone in Springfield. She had to sneak out of the house and hide her clothes in the bushes because they didn't want her to leave. She was a needle addict who had been hooked on heroin and everything else you can imagine. She abandoned her children who hadn't seen her in three years. Her mother had given up on her along with everyone else, including herself. I put her in a treatment center and she gave her life to Jesus during her twenty-eight days in the center.

Our ministry buses in people from two local in-patient treatment centers. We call these clients our V.I.P. guests. They have their own altar, and at the end of the night they are invited to make a decision for Jesus. Hannah made that decision and never looked back.

During Hannah's stay in the treatment center she made over seventy resumes. She was so hungry to change, and she got so close to God through His Word, people would come under conviction just being around her. She entered into our women's discipleship program and was our first graduate. Hannah was a hairstylist before her addiction and she kept her license through it all. She would ride that city bus across town to work at a little deli every day and never complain. We helped her get the tools she needed to apply for

a job at a local salon. She got the job and before long she got a car. She won the trust of her mother and graduated the program. She gained custody of her children, and is now a Sunday School teacher at one of our partnering churches. Both of her teenage children have come to Christ and God is using her to win others to Christ. She is a spiritual daughter to me and my wife. Weekly, I am able to send women her way for her to minister to. It is a

Hanna before Freeway (top) Hannah four years clean and sober (botton).

wonderful feeling to be able to give back to society and especially to people from my home town, like Hannah.

One time, we took Hannah to court as she began to get her life on track. She was in Jefferson City going through the process it takes to clean up the past and a United States Marshal noticed her. The reason he noticed her is because he had worked with the judge for years and had saw Hannah at her worst. The Marshall said, "Hannah? Is that you? What happened to you?" That is when Hannah got to sharing about how she came through Freeway Ministries Discipleship.

She gave him, a United States Marshal, my phone number. He called me one day and wanted to talk about being an alternative to prison. He wanted to make Freeway Ministries an alternative to prison from my home town! Can you believe that? I was a very well-known bad guy in Jefferson City. The same court that sent me to prison, was now allowing me to give men and women another chance. They were trusting me to give folks a way to stay out of prison. All those nights being an outlaw in that area, but now being a help to the community. I have had the United States Marshals bring people to me from Jefferson City, and one time they even dropped a young man off on my front porch on Thanksgiving Day.

When they called me to take the young man they asked me about transportation and I told them that I couldn't get him. They asked if his family could bring him and I said "No." Guess who brought him? The United States Marshals had a Cole County Sherriff bring him. If that isn't wild enough for you, there is more. They paid his first month fee as well. Now picture that for a moment. The very court that sent me to prison, and the county that I terrorized, was now sending people to me to help rehabilitate. They also were paying the ministry that I directed.

Tyler came to my home that day and ate dinner with my family. It was Thanksgiving Day of 2016 and he was afraid. We have all came alongside him and have become fathers to him. Tyler did really well until he got hooked up in a relationship and ended up back in prison. God is not finished with him yet, and we are going to continue to pray for him. Sharing these stories is heart-breaking many times, due to the fact that some of them may go back out into that life. It does not change what God has done or the fact that only the Lord can do some of the things that I have mentioned in these stories. Remembering the promise that Paul gives us in the Scripture "He who has begun a good work in you will complete it..." (Philippians 1:6, NKJV). See, God is not done with anyone of us yet. He will see things through to the end.

I remember a young lady from Jefferson City called me from a recovery program in Branson, Missouri. She wanted help and was on her way to prison. We ended up helping her get into a local treatment center. She was someone that I personally knew from the streets and felt the need to try my best to help coach her along. Like many people that I meet she had planted a lot of bad seeds in her life and those bad seeds will always pop back up.

Just today, I had a prisoner call me from his institutional parole officer's phone. His name is Charles and he was hurting. I asked him what was wrong, and he told me about all of the things that the state had him doing when he got out. I told him that he had spent all that time in the garden planting those bad seeds, and now God is giving him a chance to get in that garden and pull them up one at a time. The thing about pulling up the seeds of the past is eventually they stop coming up; then you get to plant good seeds down in their place. That is what I was trying to do with this young lady. I was trying to help her pull up the bad seeds and plant some good ones, so my son Chase and I took her to court.

You have to understand, the courthouse in Jefferson City is way different to me than any other court houses that I go to. I am in court on a regular basis and I go into the County Jail weekly visiting inmates as a chaplain to them, in the county where I reside. The Cole County Courthouse is one that I have been arrested in and carried out in handcuffs. I entered this courthouse with this young lady. I thought all was said and done so I told her, Chase and I would be outside. Not much longer after she came running outside and said, "John, Mark wants to talk with you." I thought, "What is she talking about?" This Mark she was talking about was sitting behind the bench by the Judge and had placed me in handcuffs more times than I can count.

I went to the front of the courtroom full of people and approached him. He said, "I wouldn't believe it if I didn't see it myself." I asked him if he would step into the hallway and talk with me. He followed me out into the hallway and I shared my testimony with him. He told me that he would have never thought that this could happen to me in a million years. I asked him if he would take a moment and watch our nine-minute promotional video. I turned it on for him and we stood in the hallway together while he watched and listened to the video. I was like a narrator for him. Sharing the stories

of the people and where they came from before they could
even speak on the video.

I was so excited to let him know that God is alive, and
people like me can change. I apologized to him for causing so
many problems in the community and asked for his
forgiveness. Then he said something that still encourages me
to this day. He said, "I walked into the station the other day
and Lieutenant Steve called me into his office. He was
watching one of your YouTube videos and he couldn't believe
it either." Earlier in this book I spoke about having a gun put
to my head and my wrist broken due to handcuffs being left
on my for hours. This was all done in Jefferson City and now
the authorities are calling me to help change people's lives.
There was a police officer who even tried to make me look as
if I told on some well-known drug dealers so I might get hurt
or possibly killed. Well, the officer that did that was
Lieutenant Steve.

Here is interesting part of the story. I felt the need to
make things right with this man who once broke my wrist. I
called him from my own phone one day because I was
convicted by God to apologize to him for the wrongs that I
committed and share my testimony with him. I called the
Jefferson City Police Station and asked to talk to him by name.
The operator said, "Hold please and I will patch you through
to him." I waited in anticipation almost afraid that he would
actually pick up the phone. He never answered so I left him a
message. The message went something like this: "Sir, this is
John Stroup and I have something to tell you. I just wanted to

ask for your forgiveness for all the trouble I caused in your community. I ask that you forgive me and hope that you know people like me can change. I am thankful for you risking your life and placing me in handcuffs because it was in a prison cell that Jesus saved me."

I explained that I found a prison Bible and that I wanted to know what Jesus did with bad guys, so I looked for them. I told him about Freeway Ministries and how I am a part of helping people change their lives today. I also left my phone number and told him that if he was ever in the area I would like to take him to lunch on me. I still have not heard from him, but the invitation is always open.

REFLECTIONS AND DISCIPLESHIP

In Acts 7 the story of the stoning of Stephen is found. At the conclusion of the story, the author of the book of Acts writes, "Then they cast him out of the city and stoned him. And the witnesses laid down their garments at the feet of a young man named Saul" (Acts 7:58, ESV). In Acts 8, Saul is described as approving of the execution of Stephen and then turning to persecute the church. Then in Acts 9 Saul is found making his way to Damascus. It is on the Damascus Road that Jesus throws Saul off of his horse and he is converted to Christianity; Saul's name is changed to Paul.

The book of Acts goes on to share how Paul becomes one of the most prolific missionaries in the history of the church. A large part of the New Testament is written by Paul. At first, believers are hesitant to trust Paul (Acts 9:36), but in a short time Paul is sent on the first missionary journey (Acts 13:4). The story of Paul is the story of the Lord taking one who opposed Him, and making a fervent, dedicated, sold out proclaimer of the Gospel.

DisCUSSiON QUESTiONS

Use these questions in a small group or discipleship setting. Answer your questions in a notebook following the reading of this chapter.

1. In this chapter the author notes that the Lord can take those who were "God haters" (Romans 3:10-18; Ephesians 2:1-2) and transform them into sold out servants of the Lord. When you consider that God has forgiven your unrighteousness and He now chooses to use you, how does it make you feel?

2. In this chapter the author shared the story about him going back to those who he had wronged and seeking their forgiveness. Who are individuals in your past that you need to go back to and seek their forgiveness?

3. When you consider your past and the seeds of unrighteousness that you so, how do you plan to allow the Lord to work through you as you weed out the seeds of evil?

4. The author shared about him being able to give his testimony to those who he knew from his past before Christ. Have you taken the time to prepare your testimony so that you can share it with others? If so who are those with whom you need to share that

testimony? If you have never taken the time to prepare your testimony, then spend some time writing it down and sharing it with your small group.

CHAPTER 24

GOING GLOBAL

Acts 16:9

During the night Paul had a vision of a man of Macedonia standing and begging him, "Come over to Macedonia and help us." (ESV)

Proverbs 3:5-7

Trust in the Lord with all your heart and lean not on your own understanding; in all your ways submit to Him and He will make your paths straight. (ESV)

The Scripture that I chose for this chapter is a reminder of how God sends us where He wants us to go. We have to understand the sovereignty of God and in understanding it we say, "I don't have to understand!" God has a way of sending us places that we have never thought about going! If I asked you to plan the last twelve months of your life twelve months ago, you would fail miserably. That my friend is the way things go when you're walking with the Lord.

Let me tell you about how our Freeway Ministries went International. Remember that meeting in Mt. Vernon, Illinois, called the Jubilee Camp meeting. In that Jubilee I met two preachers that would become dear friends of mine and one of them would be used to send me to South Africa. David Gidcumb is the man who helped me go across the ocean. David was saved from a life of being a drunk. David used to work on the railroad. He is a rough fella with a likeable personality. I think I like him because he's a straight shooter and is not worried about being a people pleaser.

David asked me to preach revival, and through that partnership of evangelism we became good friends. When he called me about Africa I was blown away and didn't know what to say. Pastor David brought this couple to our Freeway Ministries meeting and they loved it. The November's were both so delightful and full of the Spirit of God. We fellowshipped, and they enjoyed the ministry meeting. I asked Brother David, "How much will it cost for Sharla and I to go on this trip?" The number he gave me was not something I had laying around. I said, "Man, that is a lot of money for us." Then he let me know, "Come and preach for my church and we will take up an offering for your trip."

Needless to say, we raised more than enough money for the trip. Not too long after that, my wife and I were on a flight to Cape Town, South Africa. I was amazed by the power of God and how much our Freeway group had in common with the folks in Cape Town. Pastor Gerald had a church full of ex-gangsters, addicts, homeless people, and your regular church folk. They worshiped the Lord in spirit, truth, and dance. I fell in love with the people and knew in my heart the Lord had something for me in Cape Town but was not sure what.

There I met one man who struck me in particular and reminded me a lot of myself. His name is Greg Craig. Greg came to Christ from the streets of Lavender Hill in Cape Town. He was a member of a local gang, a drug dealer, and ex-convict. Greg's brother was murdered by his own gang and Greg's wife shot by gangsters as well. Greg came from a rough background and had spent time in one of the roughest prisons in the world. He was invited to a tent revival where one of his old running buddies was sharing his testimony. My friend, David Gidcumb, was preaching the message. David said, "If your serious about making Jesus the Lord of your life then come up here to the front of the tent and surrender." Greg, in sharing his testimony with me, said "I was in the back of the tent and thought to myself, *this guy must be out of his mind if he thinks I am coming down front. We don't do that where I am from. Does he know who I am?*" Before you knew it, Greg was standing in the front of the tent, hands raised, meth pipe and bag of meth laying on the altar as well. That was the day that Greg surrendered his life over to Christ.

Greg told me that everyone in that tent was cheering and clapping. What Greg did not know was that his wife Charlene had been praying for him with that church. She had started coming to the church and seeking prayer for Greg. She needed help from the group as someone who was being affected by drug addiction. The Lord showed Himself faithful to answer those prayers (2 Tim 2:13).

When I met Greg, I knew that God was going to make us become good friends, but I had no clue of the extent of that relationship. Before leaving South Africa, I told Greg, "I am going to fly you to the USA." He looked at me like I was crazy and honestly, I couldn't believe I said it. Somehow, I knew that I was going to bring him to Freeway Ministries and introduce him to our people. Well can you guess what happened? That's right! Greg came to the United States of America.

Greg traveled almost thirty hours and was very exhausted when he arrived. Greg took a huge step of faith when he left Cape Town. He quit his job as a rehab director for a men's program and stepped onto an airplane leaving his wife behind in tears. The men of the treatment center he worked at also accompanied him to the airplane. It was one of the hardest things that he had to do. When he came to the States he was looking for *colored people*. I personally would never call anyone *colored* but that is part of their culture.

The apartheid in South Africa has left that country with a mentality of classing each other in color and the African people with a lighter complexion call themselves *colored*. Greg was looking for his own people and there was none when he got off the plane. Greg was embraced by the least likely person in the Springfield airport. My son Keith was holding a sign for Greg, and when he saw Greg, who he never met, ran and gave him the biggest hug. Greg said that was the most comforting moment in his whole trip. A nine-year-old little boy who did not care about color, race, or nationality embracing our newest brother, Greg Craig.

I took Greg with me straight from the airport to a Freeway Ministries meeting, and the adventure began. We traveled around one thousand miles by car within nineteen days and raised around fourteen thousand dollars for Freeway, South Africa. I learned to make sure to get personal with your missionaries. Allow me to explain what I mean by this. Almost everyone I knew told me to put Greg in a hotel, or with a family that had a nicer, bigger house. See, my house is just over twelve hundred square feet, and four of us live in that house. There is Keith who is nine, Chase who is eighteen, my wife Sharla and myself. We got to know Greg personally and had experiences with him that made us more like a family than ministry partners.

Greg and I traveled back to Cape Town with a team of eight people. We had revival there for seven days and many people came to know the Lord. We currently have a Discipleship House in Cape Town, and Greg is the director of

Cape Town, Freeway Ministries. We support him monthly from Freeway Ministries in Springfield. God is at work across the globe now and it is amazing. I am reminded of the verse in 1 Corinthians 2:9 "Eye has not seen, nor ear heard, nor have entered into the heart of man the things which God has prepared for those who love Him." (NKJV) I am riding on a miracle and every so often I make myself go back and celebrate those victories that have happened in my walk with God. Being allowed to see the things that I have seen and being a part of what only God can do is amazing.

I was asked to be the evangelist for Lakeview Community Church in the retreat area of Western Cape Town. I have gone back every year for the last three years. The house in Cape Town is hard work and has many struggles. Being in a third world country and trying to have a Discipleship House is difficult to say the least. They are still operating the house as part of Freeway Ministries Cape Town. I pray every day for them and hope God sees them through. I still cannot believe that I am a preacher, but now God has allowed me to be an International Evangelist. The homeless junky that couldn't keep a needle out of his arm being asked to be the official evangelist for a church across the globe! How do you explain that?

Soon, Lord willing, we are planning on taking a team from Crossway Baptist Church to the Lavender Hill projects in Cape Town to do an open air crusade. This will be a first for me but I am excited all the same. We will have a tent that you can put a thousand people in and hold it in gangster territory. We are excited about what God has for us across the globe. There is no telling what is going to happen in the next year, but we believe that this is only the beginning of what the Lord has planned for our ministry. My wife is behind me 100% and we look forward to seeing God move all over the world.

REFLECTIONS AND DISCIPLESHIP

In 1 Kings 17:8-16 there is the story of Elijah and the widow of Zarephath. Scripture explains that the Lord told Elijah to travel a great distance from the brook Cherith to Zarephath. When Elijah arrived, he met a woman who was preparing to make her last meal for her and her son. She only had a small amount of oil and a small amount of flour, but Elijah told her that God would provide for her if she would trust the Lord and make a meal for Elijah. The widow trusted the Lord and in faith prepared a meal for Elijah. 1 Kings 17:16 states "The jar of flour was not spent, neither did the jug of oil become empty, according to the word of the Lord that he spoke by Elijah." (ESV)

There are many times where God calls those who follow him to travel great distances in service to the kingdom. The Lord puts people in our path to show that He is a provider and to encourage us by the acts of faith we see in other people. In this chapter we have seen that God will take some a great distance in order to show that He is a provider. He will cause us to act in faith in order to demonstrate His greatness.

DISCUSSION QUESTIONS

Use these questions in a small group or discipleship setting. Answer your questions in a notebook following the reading of this chapter.

1. In this chapter the author reintroduces his friend David Gidcumb. The author first met Pastor Gidcumb on an elevator in Illinois. On that elevator Pastor John shared Christ with David Gidcumb. Little did Pastor John know that this simple conversation on an elevator would play a role in Freeway Ministries going international. Hebrews 13:2 states "Do not neglect to show hospitality to strangers, for thereby some have entertained angels unawares." (ESV) Have there been conversations or interactions with others in your life that have resulted in God opening the door for you to do things you never thought you would do?

2. In this chapter we are introduced to Greg Craig. The story of Greg's conversion is extremely powerful. His conversion however was preceded by a wife who was praying for him. Who are the individuals that have prayed for you in the past? Who are the individuals that you are seeking to see come to Christ? How can you better pray for those individuals?

3. In this chapter the author encouraged readers to get to know missionaries. He shared about how he opened his home to Greg Craig. While not many will have a chance to open their home to someone in the same fashion, what can you do to minister to your pastors and elders in your church and get to know them on a more personal level?

4. Read 1 Kings 17:8- 16. When is a time in your life that you have seen God provide in an unexpected way? When was a time where God inconvenienced you and in doing so demonstrated that He was in control?

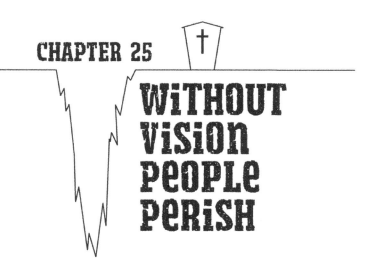

CHAPTER 25

WITHOUT VISION PEOPLE PERISH

Nehemiah 2:20
Then I replied to them, "The God of heaven will make us prosper,
and we His servants will arise and build..." (ESV)

Romans 10:13–15
For "everyone who calls on the name of the Lord will be saved."
How then will they call on Him in whom they have not believed?
And how are they to believe in Him of whom they have never
heard? And how are they to hear without someone preaching? And
how are they to preach unless they are sent? As it is written,
"How beautiful are the feet of those who preach
the good news!" (ESV)

If there is one thing that is missing from our churches it is fresh vision for our people. Every year we have a volunteer banquet and at that banquet I cast fresh vision for the next step in our ministry. My Bible is full of people that God used, like Nehemiah. God places a burden on someone (man or woman) and they cannot run from it. God places that burden or calling on their life and they respond in obedience to it. He raises them up and they are more concerned about being in the will of God than the fear of the task at hand.

Read through the Bible and you will see this: God raising up leaders with a burden and a people with a calling to do something special. Every year at our banquet I cast the next thing that God has laid on our hearts as Freeway Ministries. Our board of directors is full of people a lot smarter than me and for that I am thankful. We talk, pray, plan, and then seek God's leading for the next year to come. That next year we see it happen in the ministry time and time again. People are tired of going through the motions of doing church as usual. I know that people are worn slick from playing and want *to be* the church.

Reaching outside the walls of the local church and meeting the needs in the community is what we do at Freeway Ministries. This leads me to my next point. For over six years, we have never had a building of our own. We planted a Freeway Ministries outreach every year we have been doing this ministry. We have opened seven Discipleship Houses as well, all without a headquarters. We have needed a world headquarters for some time now but have not been able to find the right place. I have looked through endless properties throughout the City of Springfield and have come up empty. I would walk into a property and know right off hand that it was not the place for us.

One day I got a phone call from a friend that found an old bowling alley that was connected to a shopping center on the northside of Springfield. It was thirty-seven-thousand square feet in a highway commercial zoned. That means that we could do whatever we wanted with it, but it was in ruins. When we walked through it we had to cover our faces because of the mildew. The smell of the building took you over when you walked through it. I remember seeing the rain coming through the ceiling and falling onto the floor and thinking, "Are you serious God?" No one had been in this building for years except an old thrift store that had a small portion that looked like it could be featured on the next episode of *Hoarders.*

There was a pawn shop in the other part of the building. This place was gigantic; a literal mini mall that had tons of space. The pawn shop was owned by the same guy who owned a sex shop in Springfield and when you walked through the pawn shop the first thing you saw was a display case with meth pipes and drug paraphernalia for sale. At the edge of the property was a billboard that advertised a sex-shop. Did I mention I had no money to purchase a building? The property was listed for $850,000 but reduced to $650,000.

The funny thing is I knew this was the place for us. I had someone tell me some time before that they would support us when we found the right place for our headquarters. I called them and told them I thought that we found the right place. We had coffee and we worked out a deal for a loan of $500,000 for the property. You may be saying, "I thought that they had it listed for $650,000?" We offered them $450,000 and they countered at $500,000. We were the proud owners of what was an abandoned eye-sore to the community; a halfway condemned building.

Even though we needed the money from the pawnshop, our convictions could not let them stay. I told the board regardless of how much money they bring in a month in rent we cannot let them stay; they're selling that garbage out of a property that we own. The person in charge of everything logistical went to give them a notice and before he could get the words out of his mouth the owner stunned him with these words, "Hey, I just want you to know that we have found another place to rent and we will be out of the building by the end of the month."

The billboard company called wanting us to trim the hedges and Terry our logistical man told them, "Why would we do that? We are a ministry trying to help people break free of addictions like pornography and your advertising it at the edge of our property." The company told Terry, "We will take down the billboard and make it a family friendly billboard." How is that for God at work? Then they offered us a discounted rate if our ministry wanted the billboard. Today that billboard reads, "Freeway Ministries - Where Real Transformation Happens One Broken Life At A Time."

We are in the process of fixing this building up and raising the money to get it done. We are planning on training missionaries there to send out into the world. God laid it on my heart to build a wall in the building from the Nehemiah theme. I call it "The Wall of Faith." For every $200 dollars that is donated we will put a brick on the wall of faith with any name you want on it. We also got a $100,000 grant matched so that we could put a roof on the building. We see value in this building and are praying that God would see us through to create a place of hope in the middle of one of the roughest areas in Springfield, Missouri.

Today we are still raising money and trusting God to complete this building before the summer is over. Remember that fella who got on the wrong bus named Casey Merrick? I married him and his wife Jessica. She was the young lady who had the ex-husband that brought the gun to the ministry. We hired Casey fulltime as my assistant. He is helping me get this building completed. Jessica is working with my wife overseeing the women's discipleship ministry. Rick and Sherri are serving in Omaha Nebraska. Rick oversees the Freeway there and a men's discipleship center in northern Omaha. Sherri is working hard to open a women's Discipleship House in Omaha as well. Mike and Julie Aye are chomping at the bit and it is a matter of time before they are gone into full-time ministry as well. Marsha still runs the daycare and serves as Freeway Ministries cook in the kitchen. God has been so good to me and those who serve at Freeway Ministries.

I hope that this book has blessed you and my story has given you hope that no matter what the odds are against you, God can move the mountains. This is my journey, this far: *from the pit to the pulpit.*

John on the cover of the Springfield Business Journal.

Plans for Freeway Ministries World Headquarters.

John and a student doing demo work at headquarters.

Pastor Mike from Nixa, Missouri volunteering at headquarters.

Our billboard in the parking lot!

DISCUSSION QUESTIONS

Use these questions in a small group or discipleship setting. Answer your questions in a notebook following the reading of this chapter.

1. Read Proverbs 29:18. This text asserts that without vision people will perish or as some translations put it are discouraged. After reading this book and working through the discipleship material and discussion questions, what is the vision that you have felt God is casting for your life? How do you plan to proceed with seeking the Lord to fulfill this vision?

JOHN STROUP

John enjoys preaching, planting ministries, high-school assemblies, and ministering to a wide range of organizations about overcoming odds through Christ. If you are interested in John for your event, use the contact info below.

PHONE	MAILING ADDRESS	WEBSITES
(417) 616-1941	Freeway Ministries PO BOX 8655 Springfield, MO 65801	freeway-ministries.com johnstroup.net

Freeway Ministries depends on the generosity of God's people. If you would like to support Freeway Ministries contact John today.

Made in the USA
Monee, IL
21 March 2023